MEMORIAL OF CHARLES SUMNER.

A

MEMORIAL

OF

CHARLES SUMNER,

FROM THE

CITY OF BOSTON.

"Greater than the Divinity that doth hedge a King, is the Divinity that encompasses the righteous man and the righteous people." — *Sumner's Oration before the City authorities, July 4, 1845.*

BOSTON:
PRINTED BY ORDER OF THE CITY COUNCIL.
MDCCCLXXIV.

ROCKWELL & CHURCHILL,
PRINTERS TO THE CITY OF BOSTON.

CONTENTS.

ACTION OF THE CITY GOVERNMENT	7
MEETING IN FANEUIL HALL	29
THE FUNERAL	65
MEMORIAL SERVICES	71
EULOGY BY CARL SCHURZ	83

ACTION OF THE CITY GOVERNMENT.

ACTION OF THE CITY GOVERNMENT.

CHARLES SUMNER died suddenly at the National Capital on Wednesday, the eleventh of March, 1874, at ten minutes before three o'clock, P. M. The sad intelligence was immediately communicated to the Mayor of Boston, who ordered the flags on the public buildings to be displayed at half-mast, and called a special meeting of the two branches of the City Council for the following day at twelve o'clock, noon.

At the meeting of the Board of Aldermen a message from the Mayor was read, as follows: —

EXECUTIVE DEPARTMENT, CITY HALL,
BOSTON, March 12, 1874.

To the Honorable the City Council: —

GENTLEMEN, — The mournful duty devolves upon me of calling you together to receive the official announcement of the death of Charles Sumner, who, during a period of twenty-three years, has been the honored and trusted representative of our people in the highest councils of the nation.

It is fitting that the city of Boston should do honor to one of her citizens, who has always devoted his great abilities to the advancement of freedom and the establishment of just and equal laws. Born in Boston in 1811, a graduate of the Latin School, and the recipient of a Franklin Medal in 1826, he has ever retained his citizenship here, and has at all times responded, with noble alacrity, to the demands which have been made upon him in that capacity.

Although he held the position of a party leader in the most eventful period of our country's history, no breath of suspicion has ever tainted the purity of his motives; and, had his life been spared but a short time longer, I believe there would have been a universal recognition among his own countrymen, as there was among the most intelligent in foreign countries, of his wise and far-seeing statesmanship.

I trust you will take such action as will properly express our sense of the great loss sustained by this city in the death of its most eminent citizen.

SAMUEL C. COBB, *Mayor*.

Alderman STEBBINS said:—

MR. MAYOR: It is proper that the city which has the honor to be the birthplace and home of Charles Sumner should meet in its corporate capacity and officially express the sorrow which burdens all hearts in this hour of national mourning, and pay homage to our illustrious dead.

The feeling of sadness pervading our city is like that of a personal bereavement, for which words fail to give adequate expression. The life we commemorate has been a Golden Deed, and the best thought and culture of all nations will pronounce eulogies in honor of our great citizen. The American people will guard his fame as their highest example of purity and integrity in public life. His errors will be written upon the sand, while his virtues will be engraven upon enduring monuments. His memory will be cherished for that love of country and humanity which actuated his whole life; and the people he labored so earnestly to ransom will teach their children's children to call him blessed forevermore.

Mr. Mayor, as an expression of the feeling of the City Council, I desire to submit the following resolutions: —

Resolved, That the City Council receives with profound sorrow the intelligence of the death of Charles Sumner, and deeply mourns the loss of the great Senator whose illustrious career has reflected such honor and renown upon the city of his birth and home.

Resolved, That the public services rendered by Mr. Sumner in the Senate of the United States throughout a period of more than twenty-three years, and especially his wise counsels upon international questions and his untiring devotion to the rights of man, have laid a lasting debt of gratitude upon the American people; and we now gratefully recall the pride with which he ever regarded his native city, and his constant fidelity to the important and varied interests of Boston.

Resolved, That the life of this great statesman affords a striking example of the fearless and conscientious discharge of every public trust. In him we saw a man whose constant incentive was a high sense of public duty; whose heart ever beat in response to the claims of the humble and oppressed; who was the firm friend of the soldiers of the republic, whose loyalty and devotion saved the union of the States; who, though respectful to public opinion, was still above it, and independent of it; who never used his influence or his office to aggrandize himself, or to secure unworthy ends; and, above all, one upon whose pure and spotless private character no breath of suspicion ever rested.

Resolved, That His Honor the Mayor be requested to call a meeting of the citizens in Faneuil Hall, at an early day, to take such notice of this event as may be appropriate in view of the irreparable loss which the people of Massachusetts, and particularly of Boston, have sustained.

Resolved, That a joint special committee of the City Council be appointed, to act in co-operation with His Honor the Mayor and the State and national authorities, in making arrangements for the funeral ceremonies, and for such other tokens of respect to the deceased, as are due to the purity of his character, and the greatness of his public services.

Alderman CUTTER said: —

MR. MAYOR: Again has an impressive warning come to teach us that in the midst of life we are in death. The lessons of His providence, severe as they may be, often become merciful dispensations, like that which is now spreading sorrow through the land, and which is reminding us that we have higher duties to fulfil, and graver responsibilities to encounter, than those that meet us here. Another great man has fallen in our land, ripe in years and in honors, but never dearer to the American people than when called from the theatre of his services and renown to that final bar where the lofty and the lowly must all meet at last.

It is almost a quarter of a century since he took his seat in the Senate of our country. Since then he has belonged to his country, and has taken a part, and a prominent part, both in peace and war, in all the great questions affecting her interest and her honor; and though it has been my fortune often to differ from him, yet I believe he was as honest a man as ever participated in the councils of a nation. During all the vicissitudes of a long and eventful life he ever showed an anxiety to relieve the afflicted and down-trodden.

Frank and fearless in the expression of his opinions and in the performance of his duties, with rare powers of eloquence, which never failed to rivet the attention of his auditory, and which always commanded admiration even when they did not carry conviction; prompt in decision, and firm in action; with a vigorous intellect trained in the contests of a stirring life and strengthened by enlarged experience and observation, and great purity of purpose, — these were the elements of his power and success, and we dwell upon them with mournful gratification now that we shall soon follow him to the cold and silent tomb where we shall leave him alone to the mercies of his God and ours.

Alderman PRESCOTT said : —

MR. MAYOR : I rise to sustain these resolutions; but I never before felt so keenly how inadequate are words to express the feelings which seem to pervade the whole community. Charles Sumner is dead. Boston justly claims him as her honored son. Born here sixty-three years ago, when Boston was but a town, he fitted himself for college at our Boston Latin School, received there a medal inscribed as the gift of Benjamin Franklin, and finished his collegiate education, in 1830, at our neighboring university. The next twenty years of his life, till he entered the United States Senate in 1851, were spent at home and abroad, mainly in intellectual pursuits, which he loved so well that when he entered the national service he was one of the ripest scholars in the country.

Here his history becomes a part of the history of the country. The biographer who at some future day may write of the service of Mr. Sumner during the last quarter century of his life, will write little else than the history of his country during that time.

I need not recapitulate, Mr. Mayor, the services of Mr. Sumner to his city, to his State, to his country, to the cause of struggling humanity throughout the world. Though he belongs to us as a city, in a larger sense the whole world will claim him. The absolute purity and integrity of his character are above all suspicion. He was independent even of his own party (which he loved so well) and a man whose views were constantly in advance of the times. Though strong in his support of the Government in its struggle with rebellion, he was among the first to offer the hand of friendship when peace was declared. However men may differ in regard to the practicability of his views, which caused his State to stain its records with an implied censure of him, is there a man living who will dare to say that Charles Sumner was not honest in those sentiments? Thank God, that before the silver cord was loosed or the golden bowl was broken, he had the satisfaction of knowing that the old Commonwealth he had served so faithfully sent to him, in the person of one of the race he had done so much to elevate from degradation and slavery, a resolution blotting out the ungrateful words. But, Mr. Mayor, this is not the place nor the occasion to pronounce a eulogy upon Mr. Sumner. Soon his manly form will be borne back to his native city, and all classes, from the highest to the lowest, will drop heartfelt tears over his bier.

> " Let us weep in our darkness, but weep not for him;
> Not for him who, departing, leaves millions in tears;
> Not for him who has died full of honor and years;
> Not for him who ascended fame's ladder so high,
> From the round at the top he has stepped to the sky."

Alderman HARRIS said : —

MR. CHAIRMAN: I feel unwilling to suffer this occasion to pass without briefly adding my tribute to the departed statesman. Identified with a party differing in politics from Mr. Sumner, I must in all frankness bear witness to his honesty and incorruptibility. His life illustrates the success of an earnest and a laborious man. His strong physical powers and clear vision impelled him onward and upward; he could not remain contented to occupy any uncertain position. No timidity characterized his actions; he followed to the end his convictions of what he believed to be right. He was like a standard bearer, ready to lead, and his judgment and freedom of speech caused him to be ever surrounded with friends. They shared in his reputation and his honor. We lament his death, and we would recognize in this dispensation our dependence upon our Creator for all that we are permitted to receive and enjoy.

Alderman POWER said : —

MR. CHAIRMAN: I feel it my duty to say a word on this occasion. I heartily concur with all that has been said or is to be said in eulogy of the great statesman now deceased; and although belonging to the great party that has in times past differed so widely with him on some of the great questions of government, I feel that I but utter the universal sentiment of that party when I say that he always commanded their respect for his unflinching zeal and undoubted honesty. And, as I said before, I heartily concur in all that has been said and all that is proposed to be done out of respect to the memory of the deceased.

Alderman CLARK said : —

MR. CHAIRMAN; I rise merely to say that I heartily concur in the sentiments of respect to the memory of the deceased. It is not often that a city is called upon to take action in regard to the death of a statesman so eminent for his services to his native city, to his State, and to his country. The reputation of Mr. Sumner extends beyond the limits of our own country; he is almost as well known in Europe as he is here; and the intelligence of his death will be received with almost as much sorrow in Europe as it is in the city of Boston.

There is no doubt that if there ever was a pure man in political life, that man was Charles Sumner. During the many years in which he was engaged in the public service there never was any question of his earnestness of purpose and his honesty of action. In him every one who has ever felt the yoke of oppression has lost a friend. It is deeply to be regretted that he has been taken away in the midst of his useful labors. But I trust, sir, that his example will be felt by those who are now engaged in administering the affairs of the country, and that it will help to call out others who will work, as he worked, for the best interests of the city, the State and the nation.

The question was then taken upon the adoption of the resolutions, and they were unanimously agreed to, the members rising in their places.

Alderman STEBBINS presented the following order, which was unanimously passed: —

Ordered, That the joint special committee to be appointed under the resolutions in relation to the death of Charles Sumner consist of the Chairman of this Board and Aldermen ———, with such as the Common Council may join, and that his Honor the Mayor be requested to act as chairman of the committee; the expenses incurred by said committee to be charged to the appropriation for incidentals.

The Mayor appointed Aldermen Stebbins, Cutter and

Prescott as members of the committee. The Board then adjourned.

At the meeting of the Common Council, the message from the Mayor was read by the President, EDWARD O. SHEPARD, who then addressed the members as follows: —

GENTLEMEN OF THE COMMON COUNCIL: By the message of his Honor the Mayor, we are called together as representatives of the chief city of the Commonwealth, to provide such last tributes of honor and respect as are due from this metropolis to the remains of Charles Sumner. His public career as Senator from Massachusetts for nearly a quarter of a century ; his public acts in behalf of freedom and the highest interests of his country ; his sterling integrity and his matchless honor, are familiar to you all. It is fitting that this city of his birth, thi s first city of the State he has represented so many years, should pay to his memory, now that he has gone from us, its highest tribute of honor and respect.

The resolutions adopted by the Board of Aldermen were then read, and the question being upon the concurrence of the Council, Mr. DEAN of Ward 12, said : —

Mr. PRESIDENT: Although within the short time which has elapsed since the reception of the news of the sad event which has called us together it has been impossible to make preparation for an adequate expression of the sentiment which involuntarily rises on this occasion, it does seem fitting and proper that an event of this great importance should not pass entirely unnoticed by those who have differed from him in times which are passed. Charles Sumner has been before the people of the United States — and of the world in fact — for a generation. And we cannot contemplate his death without having our minds revert back to the time when the contest in which he bore so important a part, and which was of such national importance that all of the citizens of the United States were called to express their interest on the one side or the other of it, — I say we cannot help having our minds revert back to the past, to the time when, in our boyhood, that contest had its origin. I remember very well how, in the early years of my life, I sympathized so sincerely with the cause which he so ardently espoused. And even now I remember very well the peroration of an oration, — not delivered by Mr. Sumner, — which was one of those pieces of oratory which had an influence in inflaming the minds and drawing the attention of all to the great topic which was the principal theme of his oratory. I remember that the orator to whom I allude, after speaking of the wrongs of Africa, conjured up the genius of Africa, and caused it to address the genius of America; and, although it is so many years since, the language is still vivid in my mind. He described Africa as pointing her hand towards America, and then slowly raising it towards heaven, and exclaiming: —

"'I will meet thee there! I will meet thee there! Not at Philippi, in night and battle agony, but at the bar of God, under the blaze of the judgment fires, just when the highest hills of heaven are reddening with the united blaze of Africa and America. I will meet thee there, to ask for my sons and my daughters, for my kings and my princes, for my national renown and for my eternal salvation.' Slowly, like one stiffening to death, the accusing spectre has vanished. It is for us, my beloved countrymen, to lay this terrible spectre forever, that it accuse us not in the moment when the world's gray fathers and the latest born shall be witnesses of the disgrace, and the hollowness of our boast of freedom shall provoke the jeers of the world."

I say, Mr. President, that in my school-boy days I sympathized heartily with the sentiment of those words, and that sympathy is not abolished yet. It is true, that, subsequently, as I arrived at the years of manhood, I was compelled to assume another conviction of my duty, which is best expressed in the opinion of the late Chief-Justice Shaw, in a case that came before the Supreme Court for decision: —

So long as the States remained sovereign they could assert their rights in regard to fugitive slaves by war or treaty, and, therefore, before renouncing and surrendering such sovereignty, some substitute, in the nature of a treaty or compact, must necessarily be devised and agreed to. The clause of the Constitution seems to have been in character precisely such a treaty. It was a solemn compact, entered into by the delegates of States then sovereign and independent, and free to remain so, on great deliberation, and on the highest considerations of justice and policy and reciprocal benefit, and in order to secure the peace and prosperity of all the States. It carries with it, therefore, all the sanction whichcan belong to it, either as an international or a social compact, made by parties invested with full powers to deliberate and act; or as a fundamental law, agreed on as a basis of a government, irrepealable, and to be changed only by the power that made it, in the form prescribed by it."

These two sentiments, if they may be described as such, seem to have represented the feelings and convictions on one side and the other; and these two sentiments were in contest until finally the climax was reached. The war came; it is ended; and peace again reigns. At first it was like a cloud of the size of a man's hand. It spread itself broadcast over the entire land. It burst, and war and devastation followed. Peace came at length; and, as we looked around, we found the cause of the quarrel blotted out forever. In that blotting out I rejoice; and I have no doubt the entire country some day will, as indeed now does the entire North, look with pride and satisfaction upon this one great and happy result of an otherwise unprofitable, internecine war. No longer is such oratory as I first alluded to needed. We are still a united people; the cause of the division and contest is obliterated forever, and it only remains now for us to bring about that reign of peace and concord which, at the last, was Charles Sumner's chief desire and work. He entered into it with such zeal that it provoked even the condemnation of the Legislature of our own Commonwealth. Subsequent reflection satisfied it that he was in the right, and it hastened, ere he died, to carry to him the assurance that it was with him in his mission of peace. Let it be our great object now to reap the full benefit of the past, and do whatever we can for the purpose of so cementing peace and concord throughout the entire nation, that it will make us forever remain united and indivisible. The event gives rise to another reflection. However we may differ in opinion, whichever side of any question we may take, — we shall do our duty if we follow our sincere convictions. Although I may differ in opinion from others, they have not the right to go according to my judgment, any more than I have to act according to theirs, if we each believe we are right. On this deference to the opinion of the majority rest the fundamental principles of American government. I therefore, Mr. President, with great cheerfulness, favor these resolutions, and, in company with the most ardent admirer, with the closest follower of Charles Sumner, I shall take pride in dropping a tear upon his grave, and in recording my vote to perpetuate a proper tribute to his memory. I cannot, Mr. President, sit down without calling attention to the recent visit of the committee of the City Council on the post-offiec extension to Washington. Among the most pleasant duties of that committee — for it was a duty as well as a pleasure — was a call of the entire delegation upon Senator Sumner; and we cannot but remember the great pleasure it seemed to give him to have a delegation from the city of Boston — his native city — visit him. And with what eagerness he proceeded to bring forth his treasures; how he called our attention to the Bible which John Bunyan had in prison; to Pope's Essay on Man, with the poet's corrections in his own handwriting; how he brought forth an *album amicorum*, containing autographs of dukes, princes, and many eminent men; and how we neglected all others, to look upon the writing and signature of John Milton; and how untiring he was in testifying his appreciation of the pleasure derived from our visit. I remember that, as I called attention to the copy of the reports that he presented, with his own autograph, to Judge Story, in these words: "Hon. Joseph Story, from his affectionate friend and grateful pupil, Charles Sumner, March 30th, 1836," which is now on my own table, his mind seemed to go back to the past time, a look of sadness came over his face, and I could see that he was buried in revery as he was contemplating his past life, when he was enthusiastically engaged in the practice of his profession here, in his native city. There is another circumstance, Mr. President. When speaking of the appropriation for the post-office, and of some one of the congressional delegation from Massachusetts who, he thought, was a little inclined to hesitate, he said, "I do not; I am for Boston first, and for the appropriation bill afterwards." He was eminently a son of Boston, Mr. President; and as he went for Boston first, so we will go for Charles Sumner now and last.

MR. BOARDMAN, of Ward 14, said:—

MR. PRESIDENT: I can add but little to what has already been said by the member from Ward 12 in support of the resolutions which have been offered. I most cheerfully corroborate his statement of the interview and the genial entertainment that Charles Sumner gave us when we were in Washington at the time to which he has referred. In my own case — and I presume in that of other members of the delegation — my preconceived opinion of Mr. Sumner was somewhat modified. While we all had admitted the remarkable attainments of Senator Sumner, and his unswerving devotion to the freedom of all classes, an idea has to a certain extent prevailed that he was dictatorial in his manners; that, possibly, his disposition savored of arrogance. That was the feeling I had in some degree. I had learned to admire him from afar. But, certainly, no manner could have been more cordial than he showed — no greater warmth of welcome could have been extended than that by him to us. He seemed to take a personal interest in our visit there, and I wish to add something to the allusion made by the gentleman from Ward 12. When the question was asked whether he could support the post-office appropriation — especially as his voice had been the first raised at the commencement of the session for retrenchment — he replied, citing an Italian maxim, which you will pardon me for not repeating, but which he kindly translated for us, to this effect, that " a citizen is a Venetian before he is a Christian;" adding, " I am a Bostonian before I am a Senator;" creating the impression that we could rely entirely upon him, first and always. And, during the banquet given by Hon. Henry L. Pierce, he proposed to find out how the delegation in Congress stood upon the question, so anxious was he to see how the interests of Boston were represented. I do not think it necessary to allude to these incidents to convince us all of the fidelity of Charles Sumner to his native city; but it is pleasant to be reminded of them; to treasure them with memories of him hereafter. And I might also add that it was the opinion of all of us who then saw him, that his strength was unabated, that we could hope to retain his valuable services in the same position in the country and State for many years. I remember Mr. Somerby, who was there, thought he had passed the critical period of his life, and that we could assume that ten or fifteen years more of active service would be given by him to his country. It is not fitting now for us to enter upon an analysis of the character of the distinguished Senator, even if time permitted. He blended in a rare degree an exhaustive scholarship with profound integrity. It is true that in the most intense partisan strife, whenever his course was such as to provoke the warmest opposition from his opponents, his character for spotless purity was never attacked. No one could go to the Senate of the United States who was acquainted with his history — and who is not?— and see him there, constantly in his seat, constantly giving all his attention, so far as possible, to the duties of his office, without pronouncing him the "noblest Roman of them all." In combined scholarship and character he had no equal nor second in that distinguished body. In my opinion he was fortunate in his death. Rarely has it happened to any public man who has engaged, as he was engaged, in a great work for the elevation of mankind, to enter into the fruit of his labors as he did. It might fairly be claimed that his life had been rounded when emancipation was secured for the slave. He not only lived to see freedom conferred upon the slave, but he lived long enough to secure for them also full and equal recognition in nearly every respect before the law ; and, Mr. President, I think that in his death his influence will not be less felt than if he had lived to carry out by his voice and pen this same great work; that something of the asperity which was nourished to a certain degree will be banished, and that, though dead, he will yet speak in that important work. As the great Roman orator, after he had defended the republic against the machinations of Catiline, said that he " had done enough to secure his own renown, but the only question was whether he had done enough for the republic," so has Charles Sumner done enough for his own glory for all time to come. No man has ever lived in this country who has so enshrined himself in the memories of an entire race of men, who has made himself more memorable among the lovers of the human race. Never can the immortal words of Pericles, in his eulogy over the graves of Athenian soldiers, that " for illustrious men the whole earth is a mausoleum," be more fitly applied than to him. For certainly his acts, his aspirations, his philanthropy and his devotion to humanity are as comprehensive as the whole world itself.

Mr. SHAW, of Ward 5, said: —

MR. PRESIDENT: It is a sad and mournful occasion, this, that brings us together to-day. The nation mourns. To-day humanity mourns the world over. The national emblem to-day floats upon the breezes of universal lamentation from continent to continent with extraordinary significance. The electric wires are freighted with sorrow, as they convey the sad intelligence of our great calamity to the nations of the earth, and millions of people are bowed down in grief. God, in his infinite wisdom, has blotted out the brightest star of the American firmament.

In the fulness of manhood, after the accomplishment of the noble purposes to which he has devoted a lifetime, Charles Sumner has gone to his final reward. The rest he so much coveted has been granted him. His wearied body has returned to its mother earth — his soul to the bosom of its Creator. *Requiescat in pace!* But he has left behind him a noble heritage. His name and his fame are the undying memorials which humanity will cherish, through all generations to come, till time shall be no more. Possessing the capacity to master, and mastering the great questions of the day, — but above all and more than all, possessing honesty of purpose and unquestioned spotless integrity, persistent and unfaltering devotion to the great principles of freedom and human rights which characterized and underlaid all his actions, — his name had become endeared to the hearts of the civilized world, and mourning and sorrow at the sad event are not confined to this continent alone. When stricken down and felled to earth by the minions of slavery, uncomplainingly he bore upon his person the effects of the brutal assault which finally brought him to the grave; but within his soul faith and hope, and confidence in the righteousness of the cause which he had espoused sustained him through long years of bodily suffering.

> "His was the better fortitude of patience
> And heroic martyrdom."

It was my fortune to know Mr. Sumner more intimately than at any other time, during the earlier years of the Rebellion, and, while holding official relations with the Government, to have had much of his advice and counsel;

and I should be doing great injustice to my own sense of duty did I not add a few words of gratitude to God that I have enjoyed his confidence, and add something to the great volume of well-merited praise which to-day is ascending to heaven. Mr. President, it is needless for me to say that the resolutions meet in my bosom a hearty approval.

The question was then taken, and the Common Council concurred unanimously in the adoption of the resolutions, the members rising in their places.

The order appointing a committee to arrange for the funeral of Charles Sumner was read twice and passed by a unanimous vote.

The President appointed Messrs. Weston of Ward 1, Loring of Ward 12, Cawley of Ward 2, Page of Ward 9, and Kent of Ward 21, the committee on the part of the Common Council.

On motion of Mr. Dean of Ward 12, the President of the Common Council was added to the committee.

On motion of Mr. Barnes of Ward 11, the Council then adjourned.

MEETING IN FANEUIL HALL.

MEETING IN FANEUIL HALL.

In response to an invitation from His Honor the Mayor, a number of the leading citizens of Boston met in the Mayor's office on Thursday, the twelfth of March, at half-past ten o'clock A. M., for the purpose of making arrangements for a meeting of the citizens in Faneuil Hall, "to afford an opportunity for a public expression of the great loss sustained in the death of Charles Sumner."

The following committees were appointed: —

On organization: — Frederic W. Lincoln, Charles G. Greene, Charles Levi Woodbury, Ezra Farnsworth, Otis Norcross, William W. Clapp, Francis Dane.

On resolutions: — Richard H. Dana, Jr., Alexander H. Rice, William Gaston, Richard Frothingham, Oliver Wendell Holmes, Joshua B. Smith, P. A. Collins.

In accordance with the request of the City Council and the citizens, the Mayor called a meeting in Faneuil Hall on Saturday, the fourteenth of March, at twelve o'clock, noon. Under the direction of the City Committee, the interior of the hall was appropriately decorated with the insignia of mourning. As soon as the doors were open, the building was filled with persons in every condition of life, anxious to testify by their presence and their voice to the sorrow which pervaded the community.

At the hour designated for the meeting, Hon. Frederic W. Lincoln came forward upon the platform, and stated that he was authorized by the committee having charge of the organization, to present the following list of officers: —

President,

SAMUEL C. COBB, Mayor.

Vice-Presidents,

Wendell Phillips,
Charles Francis Adams,
Richard H. Dana, Jr.,
William Gray,
Benjamin R. Curtis,
George Tyler Bigelow,
George S. Hillard,
Wm. Lloyd Garrison,
Wm. Perkins,
Francis W. Bird,
Nathaniel Adams,
Francis E. Parker,
Edwin P. Whipple,
Thomas Russell,
Nathaniel Thayer,
Edward L. Pierce,
Wm. Claflin,
Thomas C. Amory,
Marshall P. Wilder,
Edward O. Shepard,
James L. Little,
Moses Kimball,
E. R. Mudge,
George C. Richardson,
Harvey Jewell,
Robert Morris,

Thomas Leavitt,
Henry Lee,
Edward Atkinson,
Joseph W. Balch,
S. N. Stockwell,
Oliver Ditson,
W. W. Greenough,
J. W. Candler,
Joseph F. Paul,
D. N. Haskell,
George Dennie,
George H. Monroe,
Lewis Rice,
Charles R. Codman,
F. W. Palfrey,
S. D. Crane,
Peter Harvey,
George S. Hale,
H. P. Kidder,
Horatio Harris,
Arthur W. Austin,
Delano A. Goddard,
Josiah Quincy,
Alpheus Hardy,
Joseph M. Wightman,
Henry D. Hyde,

Henry D. Hyde,
A. D. Williams,
Charles W. Slack,
Walbridge A. Field,
George Lewis,
William Parkman,
J. I. Bowditch,
Henry Smith,
Dexter N. Richards,
George B. Nichols,
Joseph W. Tucker,
George L. Ruffin,
L. Miles Standish,
Patrick Donahoe,
Charles Stanwood,
L. Foster Morse,
R. W. Hooper,
J. W. Bemis,
John Pickering,
Robert C. Winthrop,
Horace Gray,
Edward Lawrence,
H. H. Coolidge,
Sidney Bartlett,
Samuel H. Walley,
John M. Forbes,
John T. Clark,
N. J. Bradlee,
Peleg W. Chandler,
J. Huntington Wolcott,
Martin Brimmer,
F. A. Osborn,
James Lawrence,
F. V. Balch,

Wm. Amory,
C. A. Richards,
Edwin M. Chamberlain,
Thomas Gaffield,
Avery Plumer,
Edward S. Tobey,
Albert Bowker,
M. F. Dickinson, Jr.,
Franklin Haven,
Edward W. Kinsley,
John Cummings,
James M. Beebe,
Charles H. Allen,
Amos A. Lawrence,
Charles E. Pindell,
S. B. Schlesinger,
Otis Rich,
Calvin Torrey,
William Wells Brown,
M. P. Kennard,
Reuben Crooke,
R. M. Pulsifer,
James W. Bliss,
Harvey D. Parker,
Albert J. Wright,
George William Bond,
James Guild,
Moses H. Day,
H. G. Crowell,
John E. Fitzgerald,
H. A. Whitney,
Curtis Guild,
Nathaniel Greene,
Weston Lewis,

N. B. Shurtleff,
A. W. Beard,
H. A. Whitney,
Henry L. Hallett,
Samuel Little,
Uriel Crocker,
D. D. Kelley,
Sereno D. Nickerson,
E. H. Clarke,
George B. Faunce,
Samuel Atherton,
W. W. Warren,
Samuel M. Quincy,
Jonas Fitch,
J. J. Smith,
George A. Simmons,
C. A. Phelps,
G. W. Wilder,
G. Washington Warren,
James Dana,
H. Winthrop Sargent.

Secretaries.

Moorfield Story,
Franklin W. Smith,
C. C. Smith,
C. A. B. Shepard.

The list was adopted by the meeting; and the Mayor then asked the Rev. Samuel K. Lothrop, D.D., to offer a prayer.

Dr. Lothrop said: —

I have been requested by His Honor the Mayor, before offering prayer, to read the following brief sentence from the opening passage of Mr. Sumner's oration, or eulogy, on Lincoln. It is his own handwriting. I read from his original manuscript: —

"In the universe of God there are no accidents. From the fall of a sparrow to the fall of an empire or the sweep of a planet, all is according to Divine Providence, where laws are everlasting. It was no accident which gave to his country the patriot we now honor. It was no accident which snatched this patriot so suddenly and so cruelly from his sublime duties. The Lord giveth, and the Lord taketh away; blessed be the name of the Lord."

Almighty God, thou who livest and reignest King of kings and Lord of lords; thou who livest while mortals die, in devout submission and gratitude we humbly invoke thy blessing and the comforts of thy spirit as we gather here this morning in solemn recognition of that inscrutable ordering of thy providence which knoweth no accident, by which one of our most distinguished fellow-citizens and national Senators has been suddenly called from his high office, from the scene of his earthly fame and glory and usefulness, to the higher scenes and grander glories of the eternal world. We thank thee, O God, for his life. We thank thee that thou didst raise him up, endow him with large talents, enrich his mind with varied learning, give him a commanding presence and eloquence, and send him forth to be the champion of freedom, to proclaim first that liberty was national and slavery sectional in the republic; and then by energy and perseverance, through toils, sacrifices, sufferings and perils, to bear an important part in the high councils of the nation, and in that conflict which ended in breaking the fetters of the slave and proclaiming freedom universal and entire throughout the land. We thank thee that his life was spared till his great work was done, and that the closing days of that life were made sweet and pleasant by the direct assurance from the highest authorities of his native State that he was still held in its perfect trust and honor. And now, O God, that thou hast called the State and the nation to mourning and sorrow by his death, we pray that that death, as the life that preceded it, may be sanctified to all. We pray, especially, that his example may impress upon all rulers and people the inestimable value of that energy in duty, that firm devotion to principle, that incorruptible integrity, purity and honor, both in public station and in private life, that can alone preserve the peace, the progress, the prosperity and the glory of this great nation; and may all that is said and done here this morning, and elsewhere, tend to quicken in our hearts that faith and those principles that shall make us better men, better citizens, and better Christians; and this we ask to the glory of thy holy name, through Christ Jesus our Lord. Amen.

The MAYOR then addressed the meeting as follows: —

FELLOW-CITIZENS: The lifeless form of Charles Sumner is now on its way from the national capital to Massachusetts, in the honorable and affectionate custody of his peers in office.

Charles Sumner, the statesman and patriot, the scholar, orator, philanthropist,— a great and good man, — is dead. The whole civilized world takes note of the solemn event. The whole country, in its great cities, its scattered villages, its roadside farmhouses, and its lowliest cabins, pauses, reflects, and mourns. But Boston occupies the place of chief mourner. His character and fame are the property of the whole nation; but in his personal interests and affections he was, and is, ours. His father was an honored magistrate of Boston.

In these squares and alleys of ours, the boy, destined to such eminence, pursued his childish games. He was educated in our schools, and in the university on our borders. In his youth and early manhood, he sat at the feet of our Quincy, and Story, and Shaw, and Adams, and Webster, and Everett, and Channing. Here the future Senator received the influences from without, and kindled the aspirations within, that in due time resulted in that brilliant career, that noble and unspotted life, that unwearied, undivided and pre-eminent service for truth and right, for freedom and humanity.

Twenty-three years ago he went forth from among us to take his part in the great arena of public life — in the early prime of manhood, and without experience in affairs, yet a stalwart man, and full of intellectual vigor and generous enthusiasm. But yesterday he was a power in the land, standing conspicuous among the foremost in influence and in the public respect and confidence — one to whose slightest word a nation listened with deference. To-day his right arm has fallen, cold and motionless; his tongue is stilled, his intelligence is quenched to our mortal apprehension; his great soul gives no sign, and his crumbling body is being borne back to us, to be laid to its rest by our hands within the shadow of our city's domes and towers, and of the home he loved so well. His grave will be another added to our shrines of the illustrious dead, which we and our children and our children's children, and citizens from western prairies and southern savannas, and travellers from foreign lands, will visit with reverend steps, to meditate on departed greatness and worth.

We do well, fellow-citizens — we could not do less or otherwise — to gather to-day in this our historic hall. We come to mingle our sympathies and tears under the pressure of a great affliction. We come to renew our appreciation of an illustrious character and life, and rekindle our aspirations for the best and loftiest things. We come to give thanks to the Giver of all Good for this bright and pure light permitted to shine upon us so long, and to bow in submission to the decree that has now withdrawn it. We come to pay our tribute — not the last tribute, but the first — to the sacred memory of one of our best and greatest men. The solemn grief of this hour for the death of Charles Sumner reveals to us how much — how much more even than we knew — we did in our hearts honor and revere him while living.

Resolutions will now be presented for your acceptance, which, I trust, will be found to embody, as far as mere language can, the sentiments with which the sad occasion has filled the minds of all of us, and of the multitudes around whom these walls could not contain. I shall then ask your silent and reverent attention to such remarks as may be offered by men, who, as the personal friends or the life-long associates, or the intellectual peers, of the deceased, are qualified to speak of his character and services, and to impress upon us the lesson of the hour.

Hon. RICHARD H. DANA, Jr., said: —

MR. MAYOR: On such a day as this, when this Cradle of Liberty is draped as the chamber of death, in the presence of these tearful eyes and swelling hearts, my words may well be few. Happy indeed would be the man who could add anything to the expression of the scene. I am aware, sir, that I owe the honor and privilege of my post this morning to the fact that you and some others remember that I have been a friend of Mr. Sumner from my boyhood to the last. He was indeed a friend — I will not say faithful and just, but partial and kind to me. And to-day it is most fitting that I should restrict myself to a little testimony of what I know and remember, which is not known by the rising generation. I can bear witness that in the university his life was intensely studious; that at the age of twenty-three he had secured the reputation of a scholar and a thinker, and the respect and friendship of eminent men in jurisprudence and letters. When he went to Europe, at the age of twenty-six, he bore credentials from the first men of America to the first men of Europe, for they knew that he would justify all that they could say of him. And his great success in all parts of the Old World was owing not merely to his genial social qualities, his affectionate heart and his varied accomplishments, but there are many who know that in London and Paris and Vienna and Rome, his days and nights were as laborious and studious as within the walls of Harvard University. He commanded the respect and glad attention of the most eminent men, holding the most responsible positions in Europe. They foresaw in him the great publicist and statesman to which time developed him. I knew him in various relations, social, professional and literary, but I pass them all by for the consideration of the part he took in organizing the great party of freedom in 1848. He had been indifferent to ordinary politics until the anti-slavery cause, passing out of the region of mere moral effort, shaped itself into a movement of practical politics. It was at his chambers in Court street that that small band of men was in the habit of gathering preparatory to the

Buffalo convention of 1848. And I would pause a moment, sir, to pay my tribute of respect, in which I know that you, Mr. Vice-President of the United States, will heartily join, to the disinterestedness, the courage, the fidelity of the men who began that undertaking in those dark days when it seemed all but hopeless, and promised little else than labor and sacrifice. I recall the faces and voices — some of them have passed away — of Mr. Adams, Henry Wilson, Charles Allen of Worcester, Stephen C. Phillips of Salem, Samuel Hoar of Concord, and his son, Dr. Palfrey of Cambridge, John A. Andrew, Horace Mann — but I will not try to complete the roll. Our thoughts to-day are directed to one of its youngest, who became the most eminent of all. He has the right to have said of him what Burke said of Charles James Fox in tribute to his efforts to protect the suffering East Indians from the oppression of the East India Company : "He put to the hazard his ease, his interests, his friendship, even his darling popularity, for the benefit of a race of men he had never seen, and who could not even give him thanks. He hurt those who were able to requite a benefit or punish an injury. He well knew the snares that might be spread about his feet by political intrigue, personal animosity, and, possibly, by popular delusion. This is the path that all heroes have trod before him. He was traduced and maligned for his supposed motives. He well knew that as in the Roman triumphal processions, so in public service, obloquy is an essential ingredient in the composition of all true glory." Social ostracism had fallen upon him, in a measure which this generation can hardly credit. Although it wounded his sensibilities in many directions, it never affected his action. And I know, as an intimate friend, that it did not affect his feelings towards individuals. He did not deal with men as units, as the chemist deals with the ocean, by its drops. He dealt with them by classes and races. He raised up allies or opponents, friends or enemies, by masses, in obedience to those great laws of opinion and passion with which he dealt.

Mr. Mayor, I testify to the manner in which he bore himself during the most severe trial of self-respect and dignity which I ever knew a man subjected to. I refer to that period when his first election to the Senate was pending before the Legislature. He was tried by the advice of anxious and zealous friends, and by the hostility, reproaches and sneers of the enemies of his cause. Everything seemed at stake upon that issue. He was urged to see this man or that man, or allow such and such persons to be brought to him. It was represented to him that if he would meet more freely with those who had the decision in their power, and not hold himself aloof ; if he would say, by pen or tongue, this or that word, the result might be secured. But we who stood about him know that he was firm and immovable as that rock in the harbor of Plymouth, surrounded by the dashings of a December sea. Neither by what he did, or did not do, or say or did not say, did he contribute anything to the result. " Let them say, or think," said he, " that I am reserved, or haughty, or impracticable. I know it is self-respect. I know that my usefulness in the post depends upon the manner in which I attain it." And when, at length, the hour of triumph came, he did not allow himself to regard it as a personal triumph over any individuals or small body of men, whatever might have been his relations to them. And I well remember — it is as fresh to me as if it were yesterday — going into his chamber on the day after the election, and noticing an expression of sadness on his noble countenance. The newspapers of the day were strewn upon the floor, and he said, with a sigh: "Ah, when I see that cannon are firing and bells ringing in New England, and on the Western Reserve of Ohio, I am inexpressibly sad at the thought that I cannot, I know I cannot, meet the public expectations in this cause."

But, Mr. Mayor — O my friends before me! — could he have foreseen then the scenes of the last days! — could he have foreseen that, in three and twenty years, the news of his death would have been met by the tears and sobs of four millions of an enfranchised race; that his seat in the Senate, from which he should once be driven by violence, would be draped in mourning by the hands of his colleagues, and adorned with the freshest flowers of the southern soil! — could he have known that the news of this event was to be spread in a few hours through the civilized world, and responded to by tributes of honor and praise from more than one continent and from the isles of the sea; that business and thought would be arrested thoughout this republic, and held as by a spell, for days; that flags would be worn at half-mast and bells tolled in Charleston, South Carolina; that Independence Hall, in Philadelphia, would respectfully solicit the honor of holding for a few hours his remains on their funeral march; that the great emporium of New York could not be satisfied in the eagerness of its demand to do him honor; and that here, in his own Commonwealth and city, the entire community should unite, past differences forgotten and buried, in most tender tributes — ah, sir, — ah! my friends — *his* friends! — if he could have foreseen this, or the one hundredth part of this, he would not have feared that he could not meet the public expectation!

I have desired, sir, to contribute my testimony to some of these events now belonging to the past. It is not best for me to attempt more. If I should ever think of analyzing his qualities and powers, it would not be here and now. One of the resolutions says truly, that he was faithful to the material interests and the welfare of the State and city. This is true; but it is also true that he always made them secondary, as they are, to the great moral questions on which our national life depends. In the words of a poet, never put in print, but which fell upon my ear in this hall, a few weeks ago, whose presence we acknowledge with gratitude to-day, and whom the friends of Charles Sumner now will, more than ever, love and revere [R. W. Emerson, who was on the platform]—

> " Of what avail,
> The plough and sail,
> Or land or life,
> If freedom fail!"

The contemplation of a great character is always elevating and ennobling. His moral and intellectual nature was constructed upon a large scale; his mind belonged to the comprehensive order; but it was that mysterious power of will, that more subtle moral energy and human sympathy, on whose seat in the human frame no physiologist has been able to put his finger, that insured to those powers their highest and fullest action. But, Mr. Mayor, I must restrain myself from attempting to enter upon that field. I cannot take my seat, however, without thanking you for giving me this opportunity to add a little testimony, to express a few thoughts and feelings, not on his account but on my own. And I will content myself with hoping that the resolutions, which I have the honor to present, will not fall entirely short of expressing, in some measure, what this assembly desires to place upon the record of this solemn season.

Mr. Dana then read the following

RESOLUTIONS.

It having pleased the Almighty Maker of men and All-wise Disposer of events to bring to a close the life and labors on earth of Charles Sumner, the citizens of his native town, assembled in this hall sacred to the memories of great and good men, desiring to express our sorrow for this bereavement, and our gratitude for his life and services, do unanimously agree upon these resolutions : —

Resolved, The benefactions of his public service have penetrated to the depths of our civilization, touched the springs of our national life, and will be felt for generations in the renewed and purified organization of the republic.

Resolved, To this great result, affecting humanity itself everywhere and in all ages, he contributed not only by what he has said and done and suffered in the chamber of the Senate, but by stirring and tireless appeals, for thirty years, to the conscience and heart, the magnanimity and sensibilities of the whole people of this land.

Resolved, We recall with special satisfaction his inexhaustible moral energy, his marvellous intellectual vigor, his untiring industry, his varied attainments, the purity of his private character, the loftiness of his public purposes, the scholarly charm of his life and conversation, the dignity of his bearing, his indomitable resolution, a capacity of enthusiasm for right and indignation against wrong, and a civil courage which neither feared nor courted the hate or favor of men.

Resolved, While we unite with other citizens of our Commonwealth and of the republic in expressions of sorrow for such a loss, and satisfaction and pride in such a life and service, we have a nearer claim and more special interest as citizens of Boston, the place of his birth and home, in whose institutions he was educated, and to whose peculiar care his mortal remains are to be confided. We acknowledge the interest he always took in our institutions of education, charity, art, science, and letters, and the aid he rendered to them by his pen and tongue, his counsels and labors. We recognize that his name will add lustre to our history. And we desire especially to record our testimony to the fact that while his thoughts were directed, and his powers devoted, to the enfranchisement of a race, the reorganization of our national system, the adjustment of our relations with liberty and law, and to our intercourse with foreign powers, he never failed, as a public agent, in the Senate, to give full attention and conscientious labor to the material interests of our city, and to anything that concerned its dignity or welfare.

Resolved, We heartily approve the action of the State and the city in preparing for the remains of Charles Sumner a public funeral, in which all our people may unite, with the honors it has been the wont of our city and community to pay to its illustrious dead.

Resolved, There should be erected a permanent memorial of Charles Sumner, such as becomes a community not unmindful of its duty to its great and good citizens, and fitted to keep his character and services before the minds of future generations. We recommend that this memorial be one to which all, however poor, and of whatever age, race or party, may make contributions.

Resolved, To carry out the purpose of the preceding resolve, the Mayor is requested to appoint a committee of fifty citizens.

The Mayor then introduced Mr. Joshua B. Smith, who said: —

Mr. Mayor and Gentlemen : I would not appear here before you to-day to say a word — for I do not feel able to do it — but for one reason. I can only say Massachusetts has lost a Senator, the United States has lost a statesman, the world has lost a philanthropist, I have lost a friend.

I shook Mr. Sumner's hand for the last time last Sunday evening, at half-past eight o'clock. He bade me say to the people of Massachusetts, through their Legislature, this : "I thank them for removing that stain from me. [Applause.] I thank those that voted for me, and I tell those that voted against me that I forgive them all, for I know, if they knew my heart, they would not have done it.

I knew Massachusetts was brave, and I wanted her to show to the world that she was magnanimous too." That is my reason for speaking, and that alone. I have felt that the greatest tribute I could pay to him for his kindness to me was simply to drop a tear to his memory; but your honored Mayor was kind enough to bring me forth to show my friends the fruits of his labors. I can go back to the time when I sat under the eagle in this hall, and when I saw some one stand on this platform; and I did wish, when I heard certain expressions, that I could sink. I can go back to my boyhood, when I have seen other boys in their sports and plays, and I would walk off in the woods and say, "O God! why was I born?"

I can remember forty-five years ago, on a Christmas day, passing through the orchard and seeing a silk-worm hanging to the leaf of a tree. I took it home and hung it in the room. I put it where it was warm, and it was hatched out before the atmosphere was ready to receive it. I lifted the window and it flew off, but had to return, as it could not stand the atmosphere. And just so was I hatched out by the eloquence of Charles Sumner, and turned loose in the atmosphere of public opinion, where I had to suffer immensely. I could only feel at home and feel well when I turned back into his presence, and his arms were always open to receive me. [Applause.]

And now, Mr. Mayor, our ship in which he has commanded is still adrift. We are standing out now in the open sea, with a great storm, and in behalf of those five millions of people of the United States, I beg of you to give us a good man to take hold where he let go. [Applause.] We are not educated up to that point. We cannot speak for ourselves. We must depend upon others. We stand to-day like so many little children, when their parents have passed away. We can weep, but we don't understand it; we can weep, but we must beg of you to give us a man who will still lead us forward until we shall have accomplished all those designs for which he offered his life.

Mr. Mayor, I thank you for this opportunity. I have appeared in Faneuil Hall many times. If I was able — if I had his tongue — if I could pay him for what he has done! but I cannot; such as I have I give him. [Applause.] Mr. Mayor, I second the resolutions.

Hon. ALEXANDER H. RICE was then introduced, and spoke as follows: —

FELLOW-CITIZENS: Amid the associations of this place and of this hour, surrounded by these mourning emblems and oppressed by this stupendous sorrow, my lips seek no utterance and my heart clings to silence and contemplation. A great life has indeed closed. An illustrous career has ended. For a moment the voice of discord is hushed, and a stricken people bow before the majesty of Heaven to take the measure of the nation's loss, and to forecast the future with its hopes and fears, its joys and sorrows. It is a time not alone for mourning, but for courage and resolution also. Our streaming eyes follow anxiously the retreating forms of departed statesmen — of Lincoln, of Andrew, of Sumner, and their illustrious compeers in council and in war; and it behooves us to take up manfully the duty which they have left us, mindful that in the fierceness of battle, when the ranks are thinning, victory often hangs upon the new-born valor of the remaining few. Charles Sumner has departed. It is too soon for his eulogy; too soon for his history. Our minds are full of his image; our hearts burn too hotly with the partial veneration and love. Memory throws back to us fascinating glimpses of his person and his character, and a critical estimate of his worth is just now obscured by a suffusion of tears. We see, as it were, his commanding figure in our streets. We catch anew his genial smile of recognition, and we hear the marvellous voice which now thrilled the Senate with denunciation, argument or appeal, and again fell in the accents of sweetness and pathos in the circle of his companions and friends. In character he was a moral hero. In learning and experience he was a model statesman — the great senator. Always the friend of the oppressed and the defenceless, the advocate of liberty for his own sake, and the tireless champion of human rights for all men, his forensic efforts had the boldness and fervency of Chatham combined with the classic purity and elegance of Burke, whom in countenance he so strongly resembled. Through a long career the advocate of an unpopular cause, at times the object of vituperation and even of personal violence, no man ever assailed the sincerity of his motives, the blamelessness of his life, or his stainless fidelity. The taint of unfaithfulness never touched him. Suspicion found no lodgment upon the guileless simplicity of his deeds. He despised duplicity and revolted at everything that was dishonest. The good name of his native State was as dear to him as his own reputation; and in the discharge of his public trusts, his patriotism was the sure guardian of the national renown. No opportunity for personal aggrandizement, no solicitation of private gain, could swerve him from his sense of duty or from his conviction of the requirements of the public welfare. In the contemplation of such a character how grand is justice, how radiant is truth, how lovable is fidelity, how inestimable is personal honor! To these there is no death. Mr. Sumner, to a remarkable degree, exhibited his life, as it were, in duplicate; for while engaged in the activities of his career he seemed an historic personage. There was a breadth to his statesmanship which transcended the measure of his generation, while his learning supported it with examples from the past and pointed out the way of safety in the future. Even his conversation often bore the stately dignity of a message to posterity. With comprehensive sagacity he discerned the philosophy of government in passing events, and often anticipated his peers in seizing and acting upon results which he considered would be ultimately certain, long before they had transpired; and so outran his time, that when the world overtook him we appeared to be living only what had already been recorded. So exceptional was his greatness in this respect, that at times we saw in fancy his name already upon the immortal scroll, and his stately effigy in its appropriate niche in the temple of Fame. He passed out of this world in the maturity of his manhood, in the triumph of the cause which he had so ardently espoused, blessed with the esteem and affection of his countrymen; and his deeds and his example will live forever as potential forces in the veneration and gratitude of posterity. Thus in this world is his mortality swallowed up in life. His spirit has gone to that higher congress above, where the noblest and purest of earth sit together forevermore, in the presence of that Divine Father and Guide, who is none other than the King of kings and the Lord of lords. O grave, thou canst receive of the departed statesman only another clod of thy kindred dust; O death, thou art robbed of thy shining victory, for again the holy declaration is fulfilled, and this mortal hath put on immortality!

Hon. Nathaniel P. Banks was then introduced. He said: —

Mr. Mayor and Fellow-Citizens: The Senate of the United States is a department in which is represented most carefully and exactly the dignity, capacity and patriotism of the Government of the United States. It was carefully organized by the great framers of the Constitution and the founders of the Government to stand between the extremes of democracy on the one side and the aristocracy on the other. It is the tribunal selected to pass judgment of the last resort upon the failing men in every department of the Government. It has always discharged its duty faithfully and well, and, although sometimes liable to be a little on the one side or the other of the principle of justice it was intended to represent, it stands to us as the accepted representative of the general strength and patriotic purpose of the nation and the country. Every State has aimed to send to discharge the duty of representation in this august body, the flower of its population and the ablest of its men. Massachusetts has been, among others, most happy in this respect. It numbers as the past Senators of the State in this august tribunal, the best, the ablest, the purest of its citizens. Strong, Sedgwick, Dexter, John Quincy Adams, Otis, Webster, Everett, Choate, Winthrop, Rantoul, and now Sumner, with many others whose names will spontaneously spring to your lips, stand as the representatives of this honored and patriotic State, in that great body. In the choice of Mr. Sumner as the representative of this State, many years agone, Massachusetts, as it appears now, did a wise thing, and initiated a most important period of her history. And the distinguished Senator who received his commission as the representative of this Commonwealth in that body, looked back throughout the whole of his career, as every one of his friends knowing will confess, to the State of Massachusetts as the leader, the mistress to whom he was to look for authority, and to whom he could always appeal for support in the discharge of his duties on that principle of fidelity to justice which was the leading star of his life. He had carefully prepared himself for this mission. It was the only public office he ever held, with the single exception of a ministerial office and a delegate to the Constitutional Convention. In the varied acquirements that are necessary to the scholar, the legist, the jurist, the orator, the debater, and even the judge, no man ever stood higher or stronger. (Applause.)

He had marked for himself a course of conduct adapted to this high magisterial office. He had in the first instance determined, what I think no other Senator had determined for himself, that under no circumstances and upon no call, except in connection with public affairs, would he ever leave his seat in the Senate of the United

States; and, beyond all other men, as the representative of this State, he was faithful and true to that rule; and that, although a little thing, is an important element in the estimate of his character. He had fixed his mind upon another important point; he did not look for reputation, transitory and momentary, by connecting his name with the preparation of statutes, representing more or less the accidental spirit, or tone of opinion or morals; he had determined to look to ideas and principles, and the whole of his public life was directed to the discharge of this high duty.

He was the defender of principles and ideas; he was the propagandist of great truths. And when, standing alone, in the beginning, he had brought up, on the right and on the left, the columns to sustain his ideas in measures which he had been prompt to represent, it was an even chance if they did not find their leader away ahead of the columns just brought up for his support. In this way he had a never-ending and still enlarging and glorious field of action; and at the very moment when his spirit departed from this world he had undoubtedly conceived his future course of conduct with reference to this onward progress, to which we may be strangers, and to which we would probably, but sluggishly and slowly, come up to support. In his preparation for duty he was more conscientious and laborious than any man I have known in my time. As an illustration I can say from, I think, personal knowledge, certainly from authentic information, that when a delegate of the city of Boston, or one of the towns of the Commonwealth, in a constitutional convention of the State of Massachusetts, where the question of popular representation was to be considered and determined, he carefully studied every page of the doings of the House of Commons and the House of Lords, during the great reform struggle, in order to possess himself of the philosophy as well as the practice and experience of the world upon this great question. In every situation in which he was placed, — when, as a member of the Senate, he was excluded from all participation in the work of committees, or when, after many years' service, he was unjustly and unconstitutionally deposed from the Chairmanship of the Committee on Foreign Relations, — he had but one idea, and that was first for humanity, and then for his country. [Applause.] In these times of pretence and ostentatious patriotism, Massachusetts, ay, Mr. Mayor, the city of Boston, can ill afford to lose such a man. There is no example that leads us to duty, so bright, so constant, and so undying as this; and there is no service that more strongly claims from us recognition and grateful confession of our obligations. I ought to have said in connection with the single idea to which I have adverted, that in his advocacy of ideas and great truths and immortal principles, and his disregard of the mere phraseology or of the framing of measures in which those principles were to be embalmed, he accorded to the spirit and the practice of the Government and this country in its purest and greatest days. Parliamentary philosophy, parliamentary law, and the spirit of constitutional legislation, preclude and deny to members of these great bodies that are to participate in the duty of making laws, the right of initiating and framing for themselves the particular measures, or the particular form of the measures, in which the principles adopted or agreed upon should be embraced or represented ; and it was for the purpose of representing the great principles, and with a view to exclude all possibility of the defeat or of the success of measures, upon mere personal considerations that this rule was laid down. We have unwisely, and to a very great degree, — I might say almost to a vicious and a criminal degree, — departed from this rule ; and within my memory it has come to be held that a man was not at liberty to oppose anything — any idea, principle or measure — to which he had in some form contributed. It is unhealthy and unwise. It cannot but come to ill ; and it is a practice from which we should depart ; but at this moment of sadness it is a relief and a joy, that throughout the career of this illustrious Senator, scholar and legislator, he placed no claim to respect or to honor upon the mere measures that are placed upon the statute book.

It is as the advocate of immortal principles, of immortal truths, part of which have been executed and part of which are in the future to be fought for and vindicated, that the triumph of his life and the honor of his name must rest. The citizens of Boston have a right to participate in this honor, to assist in the commemoration of these great triumphs, to drop a tear upon his bier when it shall reach us, and to anticipate the sad moment by assembling in this ancient hall, amid these emblems of woe, to honor themselves, the metropolis of the Commonwealth, and the State, as well as its people, by the discharge of this duty. [Applause.]

The Mayor then introduced Hon. WILLIAM GASTON. He said : —

The great man who, in the fulness and completeness of his fame, has just passed to his rest, had the accomplishments and graces of the statesman, of the orator and of the scholar. These accomplishments attracted your admiration. But it is not merely to the statesman, the orator and the scholar that you render your tribute to-day. You recognize something in the person and in the life and character of Charles Sumner which he had not acquired in the halls of legislation, in the forum, or in the schools. You recognize in him that integrity of purpose, that unhesitating devotion to duty, to justice and to truth which generally lead through fierce opposition, but always lead to triumph, and at length extort praises from unwilling lips. [Applause.] You find in his character a placid and determined courage, which feared neither minorities nor majorities. His vision seemed to so reach into the future as to give him the power of prophecy. He looked through the clouds which surrounded, or appeared to surround him, to the light which lay beyond them, and by that light he saw the triumph of his principles and the vindication of his fame. South Carolina assailed him with all the bitterness of hatred; but at the time of her defeat and his victory he failed not to be just to her; and if he lived to see Massachusetts, his beloved Massachusetts, falter in her devotion to him, we all reverently thank God that he lived to see her true to him again. [Applause.] To-day Massachusetts and South Carolina unite to do him justice. By purity in the public service, and by unselfish patriotism, he won the crown, and he wore that crown most regally. A life of labor, of struggle, and of conflict has ended in victory, in glory, and in peace.

Rev. EDWARD EVERETT HALE said: —

How often he stood here and looked down upon a sea of upturned faces when they were not unanimous, when they did not agree with each other nor with him! And is not that the thing to be remembered to-day, that he dared to say the thing which was right, although he wounded his nearest friends, his best friends, and the very people who had loved him and honored him? He was — more than once — pierced to the very heart in his public life and in his private relations; but still he did his duty and said his word, and now we are so grateful that that word was spoken and that that duty was done. That homage to the right seems to have been what made the man and will make his memory. He said, this very winter, to a young man who repeated it to me, that when there was any new subject of debate, when there was any new course to be adopted, when there was any policy which seemed strange or difficult, when there were any of those clouds of which we have been speaking, when a new track was to be found and was hard to find, he never took counsel with men at last, but separated himself from men and went alone and conferred with the highest authority, and when he was assured by the highest authority, then he always went forward and asked no question more. [Applause.]

Is not that the history of his life? I see young men around me who think of him simply as an anti-slavery leader; who have a feeling that the cause of anti-slavery was the centre of his life. But he did not say so. He said that in the early part of his life he looked upon war as the great horror, and regarded this bringing of forces together, of man against man, as the thing which must be avoided, and to be put an end to, as the blackest stain on civilization. It was because he hated war, it was because he believed in peace, that finding organized war in this country, constant war between a little handful of whites and a nation of blacks, finding that in the way of permanent peace he committed himself to the great anti-slavery enterprise. That statement seems to me to be wholly illustrative of his life and method. Having got hold of the principle, as General Banks has said, having got hold of the idea, the central idea, this great idealist of our time followed that idea wherever it might lead him, and you know where it did lead him. It led him to be the beloved leader of Massachusetts. It led him to be the foremost man in the Senate of the United States. It led him, as has been so gratefully and gracefully said by one of the speakers, to be the first friend of the bondman, the best beloved of those who have led a race of five million of men out into freedom. [Applause.]

And all the time how he did love Massachusetts! Massachusetts did not always show her love to him. Boston sometimes was very cold to him. Yes, but he did love Massachusetts. Just let me read to you a little note of his, written in what seemed to be the darkest times, just before they fired on Fort Sumter. A little note of his, — why, it seems to me as if the dead were speaking to us as I look over it.

I had written to him to ask some question, — I know not what, — some list of maps we wanted printed, perhaps. This is his reply : —

WASHINGTON, 30 Dec., '69.

MY DEAR HALE: I doubt whether anything can be done this winter for ancient history. That of to-day will be too absorbing.

Meanwhile pray keep Massachusetts noble and true at the head of the column, where in character and intelligence she belongs.

Nothing can be gained by subserviency or by acute argument to find Human Freedom and its safeguards unconstitutional. Not in vain have I studied my duty here; and I know that nothing is more important than for our dear Commonwealth to stand *as she is* — precisely; nor more nor less.

In the catastrophe which is imminent I wish her to hold fast to the old flag. Pray help her. But I count upon her governor.

God bless you!

    Ever yours,   CHARLES SUMNER.

"I count upon her governor," repeated Mr. Hale. [Applause and cries of "Good."] Young men, remember that, and remember who that governor was. In these days, when we want to bring the republic back morally where he left her, remember that that great man in the darkest moment counted upon her governor. ["Good" and applause.]

There is a little story which I heard yesterday, and which I cannot help repeating here, because I see so many boys, so many young men, here who don't remember those days of dark time. It was this: That he singled out a young man not long ago, as if he knew he was going to die, he put his hand on his shoulder and said, "It is on you, young men, that we rely, and remember, young man, that character is everything." And in this last month, when in the midst of one of those petty personal intrigues at Washington, which will not, except by accident, go into history, a Senator of the United States — I should think one of the meaner sort, but I do not know who — when such a Senator said to him, "Mr. Sumner, how will this affect your election?" he said, "What? Affect what?"— "Affect your election?"— "What election do you speak of?" — "Why, next year, in 1875, the period of your re-election comes round." He had not been thinking of that at all. This was no play of his; there was nothing artificial in it; he did not know what election was being spoken of; but when he was reminded of it he said, "Oh, yes! so it will!— my re-election would come round in 1875, but I may die long before that, and as long as I live I can do my duty." [Cries of "Good" and applause.] Remember that, you boys who have threescore of life before you yet; remember that so long as you live, though it be threescore years, through all these years you can do your duty. [Applause.] Will any man of us read such a sermon as that to-morrow? [Applause.]

The resolutions were then unanimously adopted. The Mayor gave notice that the hall would be open to the public during the remainder of the day and on Sunday and Monday.

Hon. William Gray offered an additional resolution to the effect that the merchants of Boston be requested to close their places of business on Monday at twelve o'clock, the day of the funeral, and that the flags on the shipping in the harbor be placed at half-mast. The resolution was adopted, and the meeting then adjourned.

The following letters were received: —

NATICK, March 13, 1874.

HON. ALEXANDER H. RICE: —

MY DEAR SIR: Your note is received, conveying to me the request of the committee, appointed to invite speakers for the meeting in Faneuil Hall to-morrow. While I hope to be present and listen to the voices of others, I am compelled to be silent. But no poor words of mine can deepen the affection, and increase the admiration for, or add to the fame of, the illustrious son of Massachusetts, whose sudden death the nation deplores. We have been friends for thirty years, and it was my privilege to aid in placing him in the Senate of the United States, and to sit by his side there for more than eighteen eventful years. I have seen him in days of trial, disappointment, disaster; and in seasons, too, of successful triumphs, and I have witnessed his faith, hope, resolution, courage, and his tireless labors. In his death impartial liberty has lost a devoted champion, the country a true patriot and pure statesman, and republican institutions throughout the world a sympathizing and undoubting friend. He had lived to see the expiration of slavery and the triumph of the Union. But trials, and disappointments, and sickness came to him, though none but intimate friends knew how bravely he bore them. While, however, he greatly feared he might become incapacitated for labor and further usefulness, he had no dread of death. Less than one year ago, while sitting alone with him in his room, giving him that advice — so easy to give, and so hard to take — to cease from labor and take the much-needed rest, he said to me with great earnestness: "If my works were completed and my civil-rights bill passed, no visitor could enter that door that would be more welcome than death." The failure to complete that allotted task was his regret in his last moments, and the civil-rights bill he commended to an honored colleague and friend. Loving hands will complete that unfinished work, which the student will read, and the historian, who would trace the great events of the last quarter of a century, will not fail carefully to study. And, as we bear him to his burial, may we not hope that his last injunction will be heeded, and that the provisions of his civil-rights bill will be incorporated by the nation into its legislation, and that " the equality before the law," which was so long the inspiration of his unflagging efforts, may be assured to all, without distinction of race or color.

Very respectfully, yours,

HENRY WILSON.

57 MT. VERNON STREET, March 13, 1874.
RICHARD H. DANA, JR., ESQ.:—

MY DEAR MR. DANA: I regret much that an engagement previously made, must prevent me from joining you in the proceedings in honor of our late friend, contemplated to-morrow in Faneuil Hall. It would have given me a mournful satisfaction to contribute my mite to the general testimony borne to his long and arduous labors in the country's service, and more particularly to that portion of them with which you and I were both most familiar. It is now nearly thirty years since we became associated in the prosecution of one great reform in the political institutions of this country. It is more than twenty years since Mr. Sumner attained a position that enabled him the most fully to develop his great powers to the attainment of that end. How much he exerted himself during the early days of severe trial, and how deeply he suffered in his own person as a penalty for his courageous persistence in denouncing wrong, the public know too well to need further illustration at this time. Like most reformers, he possessed that species of ardor and impetuosity which seem almost indispensable to rouse the sympathy and secure the co-operation of the great and controlling masses of the people of a republic, in the difficult work of changing settled convictions at the hazard of overturning cherished institutions. The trial was a very costly one, we all admit; but when we look to see how it has cleared us from the most threatening evil that weighed upon the minds of the early founders of the republic, we cannot be too thankful to each and all of the intrepid band who took the lead in the work of renovation, and persistently carried it on to the glorious end. Among that number the name of Charles Sumner must ever remain blazoned in the most conspicuous characters. To the attainment of this great end two qualities were indispensable — and both of these belonged to Mr. Sumner. One of them was firmness, which insured persistency over all obstacles. The second was personal integrity, unassailable by any form of temptation, however specious. After nearly a quarter of a century of trial, there is not a trace left of the power of any temptation, either in the form of pecuniary profit or the much more dangerous one of management for place. He was pure throughout, and this was the crowning honor of his great career.

  I am very truly yours,

    CHARLES FRANCIS ADAMS.

THE FUNERAL.

THE FUNERAL.

Funeral services were held in the Senate Chamber at the National Capitol on Friday, the thirteenth of March, and at the conclusion the presiding officer said:—

And now the Senate of the United States entrusts the remains of Charles Sumner to its Sergeant-at-Arms and the Committee appointed to convey them to their home, there to commit them "earth to earth, ashes to ashes, dust to dust," in the soil of the Commonwealth of Massachusetts. "Peace to his ashes!"

The body was then placed on board a special train, which arrived in this city on Saturday evening. The Congressional Committee consisted of Messrs. Henry B. Anthony, of Rhode Island; Carl Schurz, of Missouri; Aaron A. Sargent, of California; John P. Stockton, of New Jersey; Richard J. Oglesby, of Illinois; and Thomas C. McCreery, of Kentucky, on the part of the Senate; and Stephen A. Hurlbut, of Illinois; Eugene Hale, of Maine; Charles Foster, of Ohio; Joseph H. Rainey, of South Carolina; Charles Clayton, of California; Henry J. Scudder, of New York; Samuel J. Randall, of Pennsylvania; James B. Beck, of Kentucky; and John Hancock, of Texas, on the part of the House of Representatives. The Massachusetts delegation in Congress accompanied the Committee.

By invitation of the State authorities, who had charge of the matter, the Mayor and the Committee of the City Council were in attendance at the railway station on the arrival of the train, and formed a part of the escort to the State House. His Excellency the Governor, and the Executive Council, were in waiting in Doric Hall; and, after the escort had entered, Senator Anthony, Chairman of the Congressional Committee, said:—

MAY IT PLEASE YOUR EXCELLENCY: We are commanded by the Senate of the United States, to render back to you your illustrious dead. Nearly a quarter of a century ago, you dedicated to the public service a man who was even then greatly distinguished. He remained in it, quickening its patriotism, informing its councils and leading in its deliberations, until, having survived in continuous service all his original associates, he has closed his earthly career. With reverent hands we bring to you his mortal part, that it may be committed to the soil of the Commonwealth, already renowned, that gave him birth. Take it; it is yours. The part which we do not return to you is not wholly yours to receive, nor altogether ours to give. It belongs to the country, to mankind, to freedom, to civilization, to humanity. We come to you with emblems of mourning which faintly typify the sorrow that dwells in the breasts upon which they lie. So much is due to the infirmity of human nature. But, in the view of reason and philosophy, is it not rather a matter of exultation, that a life so pure in its personal qualities, so high in its public aims, so fortunate in the fruition of noble effort, has closed safely before age had marred its intellectual vigor, before time had dimmed the lustre of its genius?

May it please your Excellency — our mission is completed. We commit to you the body of Charles Sumner. His undying fame the muse of history has already taken in her keeping.

The Governor thanked the Committee for the manner in which they had discharged the trust reposed in them, and stated that the Committee of the Legislature appointed for the purpose would take charge of the remains and arrange for their final disposition.

A guard of honor was then detailed from the Second Battalion of Infantry, Massachusetts Volunteer Militia, under the command of Major Lewis Gaul; and the body was laid in state in Doric Hall, where it was visited, during the following day, by a vast number of people.

The State funeral took place on Monday, in King's Chapel, and was attended by the City Government in a body. The bells of the churches were tolled, and the flags on all the public buildings and public grounds were displayed at half-mast. The services were conducted by the Reverend Henry W. Foote; and, at the conclusion, the remains were conveyed to Mount Auburn. The following gentlemen acted as pall-bearers: Henry W. Longfellow, Ralph Waldo Emerson, Charles Francis Adams, John G. Whittier, Robert C. Winthrop, John H. Clifford, Emory Washburn, Nathaniel P. Banks, Alexander H. Bullock, William Claflin, George Tyler Bigelow.

MEMORIAL SERVICES.

MEMORIAL SERVICES.

The Committee of the City Council appointed under the resolutions in relation to the death of Charles Sumner, having decided, on the 18th of March, to make arrangements for memorial services in Music Hall, His Honor the Mayor was requested to select a suitable person to deliver an address on the life and character of the departed statesman. In compliance with that request, an invitation was immediately sent to the Honorable Carl Schurz, of the United States Senate, whose personal and political relations with Mr. Sumner, during many years, gave him peculiar qualifications for the task.

The invitation was accepted, and the twenty-ninth of April was fixed as the time for holding the services. Among those officially invited by the Committee in behalf of the City Council, were the following: His Excellency the Governor, and the members of his personal staff; the Executive Council; the Heads of State Departments; the members of the Senate and House of Representatives of Massachusetts; United States Officers — civil and military — located in this city; the foreign Consuls; the Judges of the Supreme, Superior and Municipal Courts; the past Governors of the Commonwealth; the past Mayors of the city; the Executive Committee of the Board of Trade; the Sumner Memorial Committee; the President and Fellows of Harvard College; the Board of Overseers of Harvard College; the classmates of Mr. Sumner; the Officers of the Massachusetts Historical Society; the Trustees of the Museum of Fine Arts, and personal friends.

The desire to gain admission to the services was so great that it was found necessary, in order to exercise a proper control over the proceedings, to admit only by tickets. The hall was tastefully decorated with flowers. A fine portrait of Sumner, painted by Dr. E. M. Parker, was hung in front of the organ.

At three o'clock the services were opened with a voluntary on the organ by Mr. B. J. Lang. The following invocation was then sung by members of the Apollo Club.

> Hear us, Almighty One!
> Hear us, all Holy One!
>   Dark rolls the battle before us.
> Father, all praise to Thee!
> Father, all thanks to Thee!
>   That freedom's banner is o'er us.
>
> Like a consuming brand,
> Stretch forth Thy mighty hand,
>   Over oppression victorious.
> Help us maintain the right!
> Help us, O God of might!
>   Help us, Thy cause must be glorious.
>
> Help us, though we may fall;
> From out the grave we call,
>   Praise to Thy mercy forever.
> All power and glory be
> Thine through eternity.
>   Help us, Almighty One!
>   Amen. Amen.

The Mayor asked the attention of the assembly while prayer was offered by the Reverend Phillips Brooks.

LET US PRAY: Almighty God, father of our souls and master of all the destinies of men, open the gates of thy presence, we beseech thee, to thy children, and let them enter in to thee. We dare not speak of the great men who are thy gifts, except in thy presence, filled with thy love and enlightened by thy inspiration. Father, we thank thee for the character of the great man whom we commemorate to-day. We thank thee for his truth and earnestness. When men trembled at duty, and were afraid of it, he did it faithfully. When corruption hung like a pestilence over our land, he stood up above it, brave and pure. His heart was full of care for the humblest of the race and the most oppressed. We thank thee, our Father, for the truth and manliness that filled his life. We know that the character of a good man is thy best gift to thy children, and so we thank thee, first of all, and most of all, that this thy servant was what he was. And we thank thee, also, for the work which it was permitted him to do. As we stand and look around and see the prosperity and peace, the liberty and truth, and justice that so largely pervade our land, we see in that the fruit of the seed which he helped to plant; the issue of the struggle in which he lived and suffered. We rejoice to-day for him, O Father, that thou didst give him so abundantly of that which he loved the best, the privilege of serving his native country. Wherever, O God, the work that Sumner tried to do, still lingers incomplete, wherever any bond to the world of sin still remains, wherever man still dares to forget righteousness, wherever any false standards still infest the purity of public life, and falsify and retard the work in which thou didst so richly use this servant whom thou hast taken to thyself — give us great men. Give us strong, good men, who shall thoroughly know thy will and teach it to us all, and who, by the strength that thou shalt give to them, shall lead thy people in thy way. We beg thy blessing, O our Father, to rest upon our State and upon our land. Give wisdom and strength to the President of the United States, and to all others in authority. Give, we implore thee, unto him who shall sit in the chair which our great Senator has left empty, a heart and mind as pure as his. Teach all our senators wisdom, and be thyself the Governor of those whom thou hast set to govern us. And now, what shall we ask, O Father, for ourselves as we stand here desirous to commemorate the great man whom thou hast taken to thyself, the good and faithful servant whom thou hast called away? What can we ask but that our own living shall be doubly consecrated to our duties? In deeper purity, in more enduring unselfishness, in broader wisdom, in a courage that nothing can frighten, and an integrity that nothing can seduce, may we be wholly consecrated to duty, and may we lay our humble lives, like strong, unnoticed stones in that structure of righteousness and truth, and wisdom, which thou art building in our land. To some such self-consecration may we all be uplifted by the memorial service of to-day.

The following hymn, which had been written for the occasion by Dr. Oliver Wendell Holmes, was then sung to a "Holland National Air."

> Once more, ye sacred towers,
>   Your solemn dirges sound;
> Strew, loving hands, the April flowers,
>   Once more to deck his mound;

A Nation mourns its dead,
  Its sorrowing voices one,
As Israel's monarch bowed his head
  And cried "My son! My son!"

Why mourn for him? — For him
  The welcome angel came
Ere yet his eye with age was dim,
  Or bent his stately frame;
  His weapon still was bright,
  His shield was lifted high
To slay the wrong, to save the right,
  What happier hour to die?

THOU orderest all things well;
  Thy servant's work was done;
He lived to hear Oppression's knell,
  The shouts for freedom won.
  Hark! From the opening skies
  The anthem's echoing swell, —
"O mourning Land, lift up thine eyes!
  God reigneth. All is well!"

Mr. Wendell Phillips then introduced the orator in the following words: —

MR. MAYOR AND FELLOW-CITIZENS: The Commonwealth has met with an irreparable loss — a loss which it tasks our language to describe. A consecrated life bravely and solemnly ended! A great work left, in the providence of God, unfinished — the completion of which not many of us, I fear, will now live to see. We meet to pay another tribute of respect to the memory of the greatest man and the purest, that Massachusetts has lent to the national councils during this generation or the last; the one who has done the Nation more service and earned the State more honor than any other. If we measure greatness by rare abilities, lofty purpose, grand achievement and a spotless life, then neither in this generation nor in the last has Massachusetts any political name worthy to stand by the side of Charles Sumner, — the last martyr, literally a *martyr*, — in the cause of free speech and personal liberty. We meet to contemplate his portrait drawn by a master hand. No loving and partial friendship, begun in boyhood, and grown closer year by year, will hold the pencil. No State or City pride will unduly heighten the colors. And this is well. For Sumner belonged, not to Massachusetts alone, but to the Nation and the world. From the lips of one born in a foreign land and dwelling in a far-off State, — one who shared our great Senator's official labors, was his comrade in study and his near friend, — from such a one we shall hear the verdict, — the sober and dispassionate verdict which the world and posterity will render, — which history, proud of her trust, will carry down to other generations. And as long as men love justice and hate oppression, as long as they value the devotion of great powers to the welfare of the race, as long as they need to learn how the battle for liberty is to be won when fought against almost hopeless odds, so long, we may be sure, they will lovingly guard the record. As such an historian, in this sad, proud hour of bereavement, I have the honor to introduce the Hon. Mr. Schurz, of Missouri.

Mr. Schurz, rising, shook hands with Mr. Phillips, and proceeded to deliver his address, which occupied two hours and twenty minutes. It was listened to throughout with earnest attention, and was frequently interrupted by hearty applause. At the conclusion a benediction was pronounced by Rev. Mr. Brooks, and the assembly dispersed.

THE EULOGY, BY CARL SCHURZ.

EULOGY.

When the news went forth, "Charles Sumner is dead," a tremor of strange emotion was felt all over the land. It was as if a magnificent star, a star unlike all others, which the living generation had been wont to behold fixed and immovable above their heads, had all at once disappeared from the sky, and the people stared into the great void darkened by the sudden absence of the familiar light.

On the 16th of March a funeral procession passed through the streets of Boston. Uncounted thousands of men, women and children had assembled to see it pass. No uncommon pageant had attracted them; no military parade with glittering uniforms and gay banners; no pompous array of dignitaries in official robes; nothing but carriages and a hearse with a coffin, and in it the corpse of Charles Sumner. But there they stood, — a multitude immeasurable to the eye, rich and poor, white and black, old and young, — in grave and mournful silence, to bid a last sad farewell to him who was being borne to his grave. And every breeze from every point of the compass came loaded with a sigh of sorrow. Indeed, there was not a city or town in this great Republic which would not have surrounded that funeral procession with the same spectacle of a profound and universal sense of great bereavement.

Was it love ; was it gratitude for the services rendered to the people ; was it the baffled expectation of greater service still to come ; was it admiration of his talents or his virtues that inspired so general an emotion of sorrow?

He had stood aloof from the multitude ; the friendship of his heart had been given to but few ; to the many he had appeared distant, self-satisfied and cold. His public life had been full of bitter conflicts. No man had aroused against himself fiercer animosities. Although warmly recognized by many, the public services of no man had been more acrimoniously questioned by opponents. No statesman's motives, qualities of heart and mind, wisdom and character, except his integrity, had been the subject of more heated controversy ; and yet, when sudden death snatched him from us, friend and foe bowed their heads alike.

Every patriotic citizen felt poorer than the day before. Every true American heart trembled with the apprehension that the Republic had lost something it could ill spare.

Even from far distant lands, across the ocean, voices came, mingling their sympathetic grief with our own.

When you, Mr. Mayor, in the name of the City Government of Boston, invited me to interpret that which millions think and feel, I thanked you for the proud privilege you had conferred upon me, and the invitation appealed so irresistibly to my friendship for the man we had lost, that I could not decline it.

And yet, the thought struck me that you might have prepared a greater triumph to his memory, had you summoned, not me, his friend, but one of those who had stood against him in the struggles of his life, to bear testimony to Charles Sumner's virtues.

There are many among them to-day, to whose sense of justice you might have safely confided the office, which to me is a task of love.

Here I see his friends around me, the friends of his youth, of his manhood, of his advancing age ; among them, men whose illustrious names are household words as far as the English tongue is spoken, and far beyond. I saw them standing round his open grave, when it received the flower-decked coffin, mute sadness heavily clouding their brows. I understood their grief, for nobody could share it more than I.

In such a presence, the temptation is great to seek that consolation for our loss which bereaved friendship finds in the exaltation of its bereavement. But not to you or me belonged this man while he lived; not to you or me belongs his memory now that he is gone. His deeds, his example, and his fame, he left as a legacy to the American people and to mankind; and it is my office to speak of this inheritance. I cannot speak of it without affection. I shall endeavor to do it with justice.

Among the public characters of America, Charles Sumner stands peculiar and unique. His senatorial career is a conspicuous part of our political history. But in order to appreciate the man in the career, we must look at the story of his life.

The American people take pride in saying that almost all their great historic characters were self-made men, who, without the advantages of wealth and early opportunities, won their education, raised themselves to usefulness and distinction, and achieved their greatness through a rugged hand-to-hand struggle with adverse fortune. It is indeed so. A log cabin; a ragged little boy walking barefooted to a lowly country school-house, or sometimes no school-house at all; — a lad, after a day's hard toil on the farm, or in the workshop, poring greedily, sometimes stealthily, over a volume of poetry, or history, or travels; — a forlorn-looking youth, with elbows out, applying at a lawyer's office for an opportunity to study; — then the young man a successful practitioner attracting the notice of his neighbors; — then a member of a State Legislature, a representative in Congress, a Senator, maybe a Cabinet Minister, or even President. Such are the pictures presented by many a proud American biography.

And it is natural that the American people should be proud of it, for such a biography condenses in the compass of a single life the great story of the American nation, as from the feebleness and misery of early settlements in the bleak solitude it advanced to the subjugation of the hostile forces of nature; plunged into an arduous struggle with dangers and difficulties only known to itself, gathering strength from every conflict and experience from every trial; with undaunted pluck widening the range of its experiments and creative action, until at last it stands there as one of the greatest powers of the earth. The people are fond of seeing their image reflected in the lives of their foremost representative men.

But not such a life was that of Charles Sumner. He was descended from good old Kentish yeomanry stock, men stalwart of frame, stout of heart, who used to stand in the front of the fierce battles of Old England; and the first of the name who came to America had certainly not been exempt from the rough struggles of the early settlements. But already from the year 1723 a long line of Sumners appears on the records of Harvard College, and it is evident that the love of study had long been hereditary in the family. Charles Pinckney Sumner, the Senator's father, was a graduate of Harvard, a lawyer by profession, for fourteen years High Sheriff of Suffolk county. His literary tastes and acquirements and his stately politeness are still remembered. He was altogether a man of high respectability.

He was not rich, but in good circumstances; and well able to give his children the best opportunities to study, without working for their daily bread.

Charles Sumner was born in Boston, on the 6th of January, 1811. At the age of ten he had received his rudimentary training; at fifteen, after having gone through the Boston Latin School, he entered Harvard College, and plunged at once with fervor into the classics, polite literature and history. Graduated in 1830, he entered the Cambridge Law School. Now life began to open to him. Judge Story, his most distinguished teacher, soon recognized in him a young man of uncommon stamp; and an intimate friendship sprang up between teacher and pupil, which was severed only by death.

He began to distinguish himself, not only by the most arduous industry and application, pushing his researches far beyond the text-books, — indeed, text-books never satisfied him, — but by a striking eagerness and faculty to master the original principles of the science, and to trace them through its development.

His productive labor began, and I find it stated that already then, while he was yet a pupil, his essays, published in the "American Jurist," were "always characterized by breadth of view and accuracy of learning, and sometimes by remarkably subtle and ingenious investigations."

Leaving the Law School, he entered the office of a lawyer in Boston, to acquire a knowledge of practice, never much to his taste. Then he visited Washington for the first time, little dreaming what a theatre of action, struggle, triumph and suffering the national city was to become for him; for then he came only as a studious, deeply interested looker-on, who merely desired to form the acquaintance of the justices and practising lawyers at the bar of the Supreme Court. He was received with marked kindness by Chief Justice Marshall, and in later years he loved to tell his friends how he had sat at the feet of that great magistrate, and learned there what a judge should be.

Having been admitted to the bar in Worcester in 1834, when twenty-three years old, he opened an office in Boston, was soon appointed reporter of the United States Circuit Court, published three volumes containing Judge Story's decisions, known as "Sumner's Reports," took Judge Story's place from time to time as lecturer in the Harvard Law School; also Professor Greenleaf's, who was absent, and edited during the years 1835 and 1836 Andrew Dunlap's Treatise on Admiralty Practice. Beyond this, his studies, arduous, incessant and thorough, ranged far and wide.

Truly a studious and laborious young man, who took

the business of life earnestly in hand, determined to know something, and to be useful to his time and country.

But what he had learned and could learn at home did not satisfy his craving. In 1837 he went to Europe, armed with a letter from Judge Story's hand to the law magnates of England, to whom his patron introduced him as "a young lawyer, giving promise of the most eminent distinction in his profession, with truly extraordinary attainments, literary and judicial, and a gentleman of the highest purity and propriety of character."

That was not a mere complimentary introduction; it was the conscientious testimony of a great judge, who well knew his responsibility, and who afterwards, when his death approached, adding to that testimony, was frequently heard to say, "I shall die content, as far as my professorship is concerned, if Charles Sumner is to succeed me."

In England, young Sumner, only feeling himself standing on the threshold of life, was received like a man of already achieved distinction. Every circle of a society, ordinarily so exclusive, was open to him. Often, by invitation, he sat with the judges in Westminster Hall. Renowned statesmen introduced him on the floor of the Houses of Parliament. Eagerly he followed the debates, and studied the principles and practice of parliamentary law on its maternal soil, where from the first seed corn it had grown up into a magnificent tree, in whose shadow a great people can dwell in secure enjoyment of their rights. Scientific associations received him as a welcome guest, and the learned and great willingly opened to his winning presence their stores of knowledge and statesmanship.

In France he listened to the eminent men of the Law School in Paris, at the Sorbonne and the College de France, and with many of the statesmen of that country he maintained instructive intercourse. In Italy he gave himself up to the charms of art, poetry, history, and classical literature. In Germany he enjoyed the conversation of Humboldt, of Ranke the historian, of Ritter the geographer, and of the great jurists, Savigny, Thibaut, and Mittermaier.

Two years after his return, the " London Quarterly Review " said of his visit to England, " He presents in his own person a decisive proof that an American gentleman, without official rank or wide-spread reputation, by mere dint of courtesy, candor, an entire absence of pretension, an appreciating spirit and a cultured mind, may be received on a perfect footing of equality in the best circles, social, political and intellectual."

It must have been true, for it came from a quarter not given to the habit of flattering Americans beyond their deserts. And Charles Sumner was not then the senator of power and fame; he was only the young son of a late sheriff of Suffolk County in Massachusetts, who had neither riches nor station, but who possessed that most winning charm of youth,— purity of soul, modesty of conduct, culture of mind, an earnest thirst of knowledge, and a brow bearing the stamp of noble manhood and the promise of future achievements.

He returned to his native shores in 1840, himself like a

heavily freighted ship, bearing a rich cargo of treasures collected in foreign lands.

He resumed the practice of law in Boston; but, as I find it stated, "not with remarkable success in a financial point of view." That I readily believe. The financial point of view was never to him a fruitful source of inspiration. Again he devoted himself to the more congenial task of teaching at the Cambridge Law School, and of editing an American edition of "Vesey's Reports," in twenty volumes, with elaborate notes contributed by himself.

But now the time had come when a new field of action was to open itself to him. On the 4th of July, 1845, he delivered before the City Authorities of Boston, an address on "The True Grandeur of Nations." So far he had been only a student, — a deep and arduous one, and a writer and a teacher, but nothing more. On that day his public career commenced. And his first public address disclosed at once the peculiar impulse and inspirations of his heart, and the tendencies of his mind. It was a plea for universal peace, — a poetic rhapsody on the wrongs and horrors of war, and the beauties of concord; not, indeed, without solid argument, but that argument clothed in all the gorgeousness of historical illustration, classic imagery, and fervid effusion, rising high above the level of existing conditions, and picturing an ideal future, — the universal reign of justice and charity, — not far off to his own imagination, but far beyond the conceptions of living society; but to that society he addressed the urgent summons, to go forth at once in pursuit of this ideal consummation; to transform all swords into ploughshares, and all war-ships into peaceful merchantmen, without delay; believing that thus the nation would rise to a greatness never known before, which it could accomplish if it only willed it.

And this speech he delivered while the citizen soldiery of Boston in festive array were standing before him, and while the very air was stirred by the premonitory mutterings of an approaching war.

The whole man revealed himself in that utterance; a soul full of the native instinct of justice; an overpowering sense of right and wrong, which made him look at the problems of human society from the lofty plane of an ideal morality, which fixed for him, high beyond the existing condition of things, the aims for which he must strive, and inspired and fired his ardent nature for the struggle. His education had singularly favored and developed that ideal tendency. It was not that of the self-made man in the common acceptation of the word. The distracting struggles for existence, the small, harassing cares of every-day life had remained foreign to him. His education was that of the favored few. He found all the avenues of knowledge wide open to him. All that his country could give he had: the most renowned schools; the living instruction of the most elevating personal associations. It was the education of the typical young English gentleman. Like the English gentleman, also, he travelled abroad to widen his mental horizon. And again, all that foreign countries could give he had: the instruction of great lawyers and men of science, the teachings and example of statesmen, the charming atmosphere of poetry and art which graces and elevates the soul. He had also learned to work, to work hard and with a purpose, and at thirty-four, when he first appeared conspicuously before the people, he could already point to many results of his labor.

But his principal work had been an eager accumulation of knowledge in his own mind, an accumulation most extraordinary in its scope and variety. His natural inclination to search for fundamental principles and truths had been favored by his opportunities, and all his industry in collecting knowledge became subservient to the building up of his ideals. Having not been tossed and jostled through the school of want and adversity, he lacked, what that school is best apt to develop,—keen, practical instincts, sharpened by early struggles, and that sober appreciation of the realities and possibilities of the times which is forced upon men by a hard contact with the world. He judged life from the stillness of the student's closet and from his intercourse with the refined and elevated, and he acquired little of those experiences which might have dampened his zeal in working for his ideal aims, and staggered his faith in their realization. His mind loved to move and operate in the realm of ideas, not of things; in fact, it could scarcely have done otherwise. Thus nature and education made him an idealist,— and, indeed, he stands as the most pronounced idealist among the public men of America.

He was an ardent friend of liberty, not like one of those who have themselves suffered oppression and felt the galling weight of chains; nor like those who in the common walks of life have experienced the comfort of wide elbow-room and the quickening and encouraging influence of free institutions for the practical work of society. But to him liberty was the ideal goddess clothed in sublime attributes of surpassing beauty and beneficence, giving to every human being his eternal rights, showering around her the treasures of her blessings, and lifting up the lowly to an ideal existence.

In the same ethereal light stood in his mind the republic, his country, the law, the future organization of the great family of nations.

That idealism was sustained and quickened, not merely by his vast learning and classical inspirations, but by that rare and exquisite purity of life, and high moral sensitiveness, which he had preserved intact and fresh through all the temptations of his youth, and which remained intact and fresh down to his last day.

Such was the man, when, in the exuberant vigor of manhood, he entered public life. Until that time he had entertained no aspirations for a political career. When discussing with a friend of his youth — now a man of fame, — what the future might have in store for them, he said: "You may be a Senator of the United States some day; but nothing would make me happier than to be President of Harvard College."

And in later years he publicly declared: "With the ample opportunities of private life I was content. No tombstone for me could bear a fairer inscription than this: 'Here lies one who, without the honors or emoluments of public station, did something for his fellow-men.'" It was the scholar who spoke, and no doubt he spoke sincerely. But he found the slavery question in his path; or, rather, the slavery question seized upon him. The advocate of universal peace, of the eternal reign of justice and charity, could not fail to see in slavery the embodiment of universal war of man against man, of absolute injustice and oppression. Little knowing where the first word would carry him, he soon found himself in the midst of the struggle.

The idealist found a living question to deal with, which, like a flash of lightning, struck into the very depth of his soul, and set it on fire. The whole ardor of his nature broke out in the enthusiasm of the anti-slavery man. In a series of glowing addresses and letters he attacked the great wrong. He protested against the Mexican war; he assailed with powerful strokes the fugitive slave law; he attempted to draw the Whig party into a decided anti-slavery policy; and when that failed, he broke through his party affiliations, and joined the small band of Free Soilers. He was an abolitionist by nature, but not one of those who rejected the Constitution as a covenant with slavery. His legal mind found in the Constitution no express recognition of slavery, and he consistently construed it as a warrant of freedom. This placed him in the ranks of those who were called "political abolitionists."

He did not think of the sacrifices which this obedience to his moral impulses might cost him. For, at that time, abolitionism was by no means a fashionable thing. An anti-slavery man was then, even in Boston, positively the horror of a large portion of polite society. To make anti-slavery speeches was looked upon, not only as an incendiary, but a vulgar occupation. And that the highly refined Sumner, who was so learned and able, who had seen the world and mixed with the highest social circles in Europe; who knew the classics by heart, and could deliver judgment on a picture or a statue like a veteran connoisseur; who was a favorite with the wealthy and powerful, and could in his aspirations for an easy and fitting position in life count upon their whole influence, if he only would not do anything foolish, — that such a man should go among the abolitionists, and not only sympathize with them, but work with them, and expose himself to the chance of being dragged through the streets by vulgar hands with a rope round his neck, like William Lloyd Garrison, — that was a thing at which the polite society of that day would revolt, and which no man could undertake without danger of being severely dropped. But that was the thing which the refined Sumner actually did, probably without giving a moment's thought to the possible consequences.

He went even so far as openly to defy that dictatorship which Daniel Webster had for so many years been exercising over the political mind of Massachusetts, and which then was about to exert its power in favor of a compromise with slavery.

But times were changing, and only six years after the delivery of his first popular address he was elected to the Senate of the United States by a combination of Democrats and Free-Soilers.

Charles Sumner entered the Senate on the 1st day of December, 1851. He entered as the successor of Daniel Webster, who had been appointed Secretary of State. On that same 1st of December Henry Clay spoke his last word in the Senate, and then left the chamber, never to return.

A striking and most significant coincidence: Henry Clay disappeared from public life; Daniel Webster left the

Senate, drawing near his end; Charles Sumner stepped upon the scene. The close of one and the setting in of another epoch in the history of the American Republic were portrayed in the exit and entry of these men.

Clay and Webster had appeared in the councils of the nation in the early part of this century. The Republic was then still in its childhood, in almost every respect still an untested experiment, an unsolved problem. Slowly and painfully had it struggled through the first conflicts of constitutional theories, and acquired only an uncertain degree of national consistency. There were the somewhat unruly democracies of the States, with their fresh revolutionary reminiscences, their instincts of entirely independent sovereignty, and their now and then seemingly divergent interests; and the task of binding them firmly together in the bonds of common aspirations, of national spirit and the authority of national law, had, indeed, fairly progressed, but was far from being entirely accomplished. The United States, not yet compacted by the means of rapid locomotion which to-day make every inhabitant of the land a neighbor of the national capital, were then still a straggling confederacy; and the members of that confederacy had, since the triumphant issue of the Revolution, more common memories of severe trials, sufferings, embarrassments, dangers and anxieties together, than of cheering successes and of assured prosperity and well-being.

The great powers of the Old World, fiercely contending among themselves for the mastery, trampled, without remorse, upon the neutral rights of the young and feeble Republic. A war was impending with one of them, bringing on disastrous reverses and spreading alarm and discontent over the land. A dark cloud of financial difficulty hung over the nation. And the danger from abroad and embarrassments at home were heightened by a restless party spirit, which former disagreements had left behind them, and which every newly-arising question seemed to embitter. The outlook was dark and uncertain. It was under such circumstances that Henry Clay first, and Daniel Webster shortly after him, stepped upon the scene, and at once took their station in the foremost rank of public men.

The problems to be solved by the statesmen of that period were of an eminently practical nature. They had to establish the position of the young Republic among the powers of the earth; to make her rights as a neutral respected; to secure the safety of her maritime interests. They had to provide for national defence. They had to set the interior household of the Republic in working order.

They had to find remedies for a burdensome public debt and a disordered currency. They had to invent and originate policies, to bring to light the resources of the land, sleeping unknown in the virgin soil; to open and make accessible to the husbandman the wild acres yet untouched; to protect the frontier settler against the inroads of the savage; to call into full activity the agricultural, commercial and industrial energies of the people; to develop and extend the prosperity of the nation so as to make even the discontented cease to doubt that the national union was, and should be maintained as, a blessing to all.

Thus we find the statesmanship of those times busily occupied with practical detail of foreign policy, national defence, financial policy, tariffs, banks, organization of governmental departments, land policy, Indian policy, internal improvements, settlements of disputes and difficulties among the States, contrivances of expediency of all sorts, to put the Government firmly upon its feet, and to set and keep in orderly motion the working of the political machinery, to build up and strengthen and secure the framework in which the mighty developments of the future were to take place.

Such a task, sometimes small in its details, but difficult and grand in its comprehensiveness, required that creative, organizing, building kind of statesmanship, which to large and enlightened views of the aims and ends of political organization and of the wants of society must add a practical knowledge of details, a skilful handling of existing material, a just understanding of causes and effects, the ability to compose distracting conflicts and to bring the social forces into fruitful co-operation.

On this field of action Clay and Webster stood in the front rank of an illustrious array of contemporaries: Clay, the originator of measures and policies, with his inventive and organizing mind, not rich in profound ideas or in knowledge gathered by book study, but learning as he went; quick in the perception of existing wants and difficulties and of the means within reach to satisfy the one and overcome the other; and a born captain also, — a commander of men, who appeared as if riding through the struggles of those days mounted on a splendidly caparisoned charger, sword in hand, and with waving helmet and plume, leading the front; — a fiery and truly magnetic soul, overawing with his frown, enchanting with his smile, flourishing the weapon of eloquence like a wizard's wand, overwhelming opposition and kindling and fanning the flame of enthusiasm; — a marshaller of parties, whose very presence and voice like a signal blast created and wielded organization.

And by his side Daniel Webster, with that awful vastness of brain, a tremendous storehouse of thought and knowledge, which gave forth its treasures with ponderous majesty of utterance; he not an originator of measures and policies, but a mighty advocate, the greatest advocate this country ever knew, — a king in the realm of intellect, and the solemn embodiment of authority, — a huge Atlas, who carried the constitution on his shoulders. He could have carried there the whole moral grandeur of the nation, had he never compromised his own.

Such men filled the stage during that period of construction and conservative national organization, devoting the best efforts of their statesmanship, the statesmanship of the political mind, to the purpose of raising their country to greatness in wealth and power, of making the people proud of their common nationality, and of imbedding the Union in the contentment of prosperity, in enlightened patriotism, national law, and constitutional principle.

And when they drew near their end, they could boast of many a grand achievement, not indeed exclusively their own, for other powerful minds had their share in the work. The United States stood there among the great powers of the earth, strong and respected. The Republic had no foreign foe to fear; its growth in population and wealth, in popular intelligence and progressive civilization, the wonder of the world. There was no visible limit to its development; there seemed to be no danger to its integrity.

But among the problems which the statesmen of that period had grappled with, there was one which had eluded their grasp. Many a conflict of opinion and interest they had succeeded in settling, either by positive decision, or by judicious composition. But one conflict had stubbornly baffled the statesmanship of expedients, for it was more than a mere conflict of opinion and interest. It was a conflict grounded deep in the moral nature of men — the slavery question.

Many a time had it appeared on the surface during the period I have described, threatening to overthrow all that had been ingeniously built up, and to break asunder all that had been laboriously cemented together. In their anxiety to avert every danger threatening the Union, they attempted to repress the slavery question by compromise, and, apparently, with success, at least for a while.

But however firmly those compromises seemed to stand, there was a force of nature at work which, like a restless flood, silently but unceasingly and irresistibly washed their foundation away, until at last the towering structure toppled down.

The anti-slavery movement is now one of the great chapters of our past history. The passions of the struggle having been buried in thousands of graves, and the victory of Universal Freedom standing as firm and unquestionable as the eternal hills, we may now look back upon that history with an impartial eye. It may be hoped that even the people of the South, if they do not yet appreciate the spirit which created and guided the anti-slavery movement, will not much longer misunderstand it. Indeed, they grievously misunderstood it at the time. They looked upon it as the offspring of a wanton desire to meddle with other people's affairs, or as the product of hypocritical selfishness assuming the mask and cant of philanthropy, merely to rob the South and to enrich New England; or as an insidious contrivance of criminally reckless political ambition, striving to grasp and monopolize power at the risk of destroying a part of the country or even the whole.

It was, perhaps, not unnatural that those interested in slavery should have thought so; but from this great error arose their fatal miscalculation as to the peculiar strength of the anti-slavery cause.

No idea ever agitated the popular mind to whose origin calculating selfishness was more foreign. Even the great uprising which brought about the War of Independence was less free from selfish motives, for it sprang from resistance to a tyrannical abuse of the taxing power. Then the people rose against that oppression which touched their property; the anti-slavery movement originated in an impulse purely moral.

It was the irresistible breaking out of a trouble of conscience,— a trouble of conscience which had already disturbed the men who made the American Republic. It found a voice in their anxious admonitions, their gloomy prophecies, their scrupulous care to exclude from the Constitution all forms of expression which might have appeared to sanction the idea of property in man.

It found a voice in the fierce struggles which resulted in the Missouri compromise. It was repressed for a time by material interest, by the greed of gain, when the peculiar product of slave labor became one of the principal staples of the country and a mine of wealth. But the trouble of conscience raised its voice again, shrill and defiant as when your own John Quincy Adams stood in the halls of Congress, and when devoted advocates of the rights of man began and carried on, in the face of ridicule and brutal persecution, an agitation seemingly hopeless. It cried out again and again, until at last its tones and echoes grew louder than all the noises that were to drown it.

The anti-slavery movement found arrayed against itself all the influences, all the agencies, all the arguments which ordinarily control the actions of men.

Commerce said, — Do not disturb slavery, for its products fill our ships and are one of the principal means of our exchanges. Industry said, — Do not disturb slavery, for it feeds our machinery and gives us markets. The greed of wealth said, — Do not disturb slavery, for it is an inexhaustible fountain of riches. Political ambition said, — Do not disturb slavery, for it furnishes us combinations and compromises to keep parties alive and to make power the price of shrewd management. An anxious statesmanship said, — Do not disturb slavery, for you might break to pieces the union of these States.

There never was a more formidable combination of interests and influences than that which confronted the anti-slavery movement in its earlier stages. And what was its answer? "Whether all you say be true or false, it matters not, but slavery is wrong."

Slavery is wrong! That one word was enough. It stood there like a huge rock in the sea, shivering to spray the waves dashing upon it. Interest, greed, argument, vituperation, calumny, ridicule, persecution, patriotic appeal, — it was all in vain. Amidst all the storm and assault that one word stood there unmoved, intact and impregnable: Slavery is wrong.

Such was the vital spirit of the anti-slavery movement in its early development. Such a spirit alone could inspire that religious devotion which gave to the believer all the stubborn energy of fanaticism; it alone could kindle that deep enthusiasm which made men willing to risk and sacrifice everything for a great cause; it alone could keep alive that unconquerable faith in the certainty of ultimate success which boldly attempted to overcome seeming impossibilities.

It was indeed a great spirit, as, against difficulties which threw pusillanimity into despair, it painfully struggled into light, often baffled and as often pressing forward with devotion always fresh; nourished by nothing but a profound sense of right; encouraged by nothing but the cheering sympathy of liberty-loving mankind the world over, and by the hope that some day the conscience of the American people would be quickened by a full understanding of the dangers which the existence of the great wrong would bring upon the Republic. No scramble for the spoils of office then, no expectation of a speedy conquest of power, — nothing but that conviction, that enthusiasm, that faith in the breasts of a small band of men, and the prospect of new uncertain struggles and trials.

At the time when Mr. Sumner entered the Senate, the hope of final victory appeared as distant as ever; but it only appeared so. The statesmen of the past period had just succeeded in building up that compromise which admitted California as a free State, and imposed upon the Republic the fugitive slave law. That compromise, like all its predecessors, was considered and called a final settlement. The two great political parties accepted it as such. In whatever they might differ, as to this they solemnly proclaimed their agreement. Fidelity to it was looked upon as a test of true patriotism, and as a qualification necessary for the possession of political power. Opposition to it was denounced as factious, unpatriotic, revolutionary demagogism, little short of treason. An overwhelming majority of the American people acquiesced in it. Material interest looked upon it with satisfaction, as a promise of repose; timid and sanguine patriots greeted it as a new bond of union; politicians hailed it as an assurance that the fight for the public plunder might be carried on without the disturbing intrusion of a moral principle in politics. But, deep down, men's conscience like a volcanic fire was restless, ready for a new outbreak as soon as the thin crust of compromise should crack. And just then the day was fast approaching when the moral idea, which so far had only broken out sporadically, and moved small numbers of men to open action, should receive a reinforcement strong enough to transform a forlorn hope into an army of irresistible strength. One of those eternal laws which govern the development of human affairs asserted itself, — the law that a great wrong, which has been maintained in defiance of the moral sense of mankind, must finally, by the very means and measures necessary for its sustenance, render itself so insupportable as to insure its downfall and destruction.

So it was with slavery. I candidly acquit the American slave-power of wilful and wanton aggression upon the liberties and general interests of the American people. If slavery was to be kept alive at all, its supporters could not act otherwise than they did.

Slavery could not live and thrive in an atmosphere of free inquiry and untrammelled discussion. Therefore free inquiry and discussion touching slavery had to be suppressed.

Slavery could not be secure, if slaves, escaping merely across a State line, thereby escaped the grasp of their masters. Hence an effective fugitive slave law was imperatively demanded.

Slavery could not protect its interests in the Union unless its power balanced that of the free States in the national councils. Therefore by colonization or conquest the number of slave States had to be augmented. Hence the annexation of Texas, the Mexican war, and intrigues for the acquisition of Cuba.

Slavery could not maintain the equilibrium of power, if it permitted itself to be excluded from the national Territories. Hence the breaking down of the Missouri Compromise and the usurpation in Kansas.

Thus slavery was pushed on and on by the inexorable logic of its existence; the slave masters were only the slaves of the necessities of slavery, and all their seeming exactions and usurpations were merely a struggle for its life.

Many of their demands had been satisfied, on the part of the North, by submission or compromise. The Northern people, although with reluctant conscience, had acquiesced in the contrivances of politicians, for the sake of peace. But when the slave-power went so far as to demand for slavery the great domain of the nation which had been held sacred to freedom forever, then the people of the North suddenly understood that the necessities of slavery demanded what they could not yield. Then the conscience of the masses was relieved of the doubts and fears which had held it so long in check; their moral impulses were quickened by practical perceptions; the moral idea became a practical force, and the final struggle began. It was made inevitable by the necessities of slavery; it was indeed an irrepressible conflict.

These things were impending when Henry Clay and Daniel Webster, the architects of the last compromise, left the Senate. Had they, with all their far-seeing statesmanship, never understood this logic of things? When they made their compromises, did they only desire to postpone the final struggle, until they should be gone, so that they might not witness the terrible concussion? Or had their great and manifold achievements with the statesmanship of organization and expediency so deluded their minds, that they really hoped a compromise which only ignored, but did not settle, the great moral question, could furnish an enduring basis for future developments?

One thing they and their contemporaries had indeed accomplished; under their care the Republic had grown so great and strong, its vitality had become so tough, that it could endure the final struggle without falling to pieces under its shocks.

Whatever their errors, their delusions, and, perhaps, their misgivings may have been, this they had accomplished; and then they left the last compromise tottering behind them, and turned their faces to the wall and died.

And with them stepped into the background the statesmanship of organization, expedients and compromises; and to the front came, ready for action, the moral idea which was to fight out the great conflict, and to open a new epoch of American history.

That was the historic significance of the remarkable scene which showed us Henry Clay walking out of the Senate Chamber never to return, when Charles Sumner sat down there as the successor of Daniel Webster.

No man could, in his whole being, have more strikingly portrayed that contrast. When Charles Sumner had been elected to the Senate, Theodore Parker said to him, in a letter of congratulation, "You told me once that you were in morals, not in politics. Now I hope you will show that you are still in morals, although in politics. I hope you will be the senator with a conscience." That hope was gratified. He always remained in morals while in politics. He never was anything else but the senator with a conscience. Charles Sumner entered the Senate not as a mere advocate, but as the very embodiment of the moral idea. From this fountain flowed his highest aspirations. There had been great anti-slavery men in the Senate before him; they were there with him, men like Seward and Chase. But they had been trained in a different school. Their minds had ranged over other political fields. They understood politics. He did not. He knew but one political object, — to combat and overthrow the great wrong of slavery ; to serve the ideal of the liberty and equality of men ; and to establish the universal reign of "peace, justice and charity." He brought to the Senate a studious mind, vast learning, great legal attainments, a powerful eloquence, a strong and ardent nature ; and all this he vowed to one service. With all this he was not a mere expounder of a policy ; he was a worshipper, sincere and devout, at the shrine of his ideal. In no public man had the moral idea of the anti-slavery movement more overruling strength. He made everything yield to it. He did not possess it; it possessed him. That was the secret of his peculiar power.

He introduced himself into the debates of the Senate, the slavery question having been silenced forever, as politicians then thought, by several speeches on other subjects, — the reception of Kossuth, the Land Policy, Ocean Postage; but they were not remarkable, and attracted but little attention.

At last he availed himself of an appropriation bill to attack the fugitive slave law, and at once a spirit broke forth in that first word on the great question which startled every listener.

Thus he opened the argument: —

"Painfully convinced of the unutterable wrong and woe of slavery,— profoundly believing that according to the true spirit of the Constitution and the sentiments of the fathers, it can find no place under our national government,— I could not allow this session to reach its close without making or seizing an opportunity to declare myself openly against the usurpation, injustice, and cruelty of the late intolerant enactment for the recovery of fugitive slaves."

Then this significant declaration: —

"Whatever I am or may be, I freely offer to this cause. I have never been a politician. The slave of principles, I call no party master. By sentiment, education, and conviction, a friend of Human Rights in their utmost expansion, I have ever most sincerely embraced the Democratic idea — not, indeed, as represented or professed by any party, but according to its real significance, as transfigured in the Declaration of Independence, and in the injunctions of Christianity. In this idea I see no narrow advantage merely for individuals or classes, but the sovereignty of the people, and the greatest happiness of all secured by equal laws."

A vast array of historical research and of legal argument was then called up to prove the sectionalism of slavery, the nationalism of freedom, and the unconstitutionality of the fugitive slave act, followed by this bold declaration: "By the Supreme Law, which commands me to do no injustice, by the comprehensive Christian Law of Brotherhood, by the Constitution I have sworn to support, I am bound to disobey this law." And the speech closed with this solemn quotation: "Beware of the groans of wounded souls, since the inward sore will at length break out. Oppress not to the utmost a single heart; for a solitary sigh has power to overturn a whole world."

The amendment to the appropriation bill moved by Mr.

Sumner received only four votes of fifty-one. But every hearer had been struck by the words spoken as something different from the tone of other anti-slavery speeches delivered in those halls. Southern Senators, startled at the peculiarity of the speech, called it, in reply, "the most extraordinary language they had ever listened to." Mr. Chase, supporting Sumner in debate, spoke of it, "as marking a new era in American history, when the anti-slavery idea ceased to stand on the defensive and was boldly advancing to the attack."

Indeed, it had that significance. There stood up in the Senate a man who was no politician; but who, on the highest field of politics, with a concentrated intensity of feeling and purpose never before witnessed there, gave expression to a moral impulse, which, although sleeping perhaps for a time, certainly existed in the popular conscience, and which, once become a political force, could not fail to produce a great revolution.

Charles Sumner possessed all the instincts, the courage, the firmness and the faith of the devotee of a great idea. In the Senate he was a member of a feeble minority, so feeble, indeed, as to be to the ruling power a mere subject of derision; and for the first three years of his service without organized popular support. The slaveholders had been accustomed to put the metal of their northern opponents to a variety of tests. Many a hot anti-slavery zeal had cooled under the social blandishments with which the South knew so well how to impregnate the atmosphere of the national capital, and many a high courage had given way before the haughty assumption and fierce menace of Southern men in Congress. Mr. Sumner had to pass that ordeal. He was at first petted and flattered by Southern society, but, fond as he was of the charms of social intercourse, and accessible to demonstrative appreciation, no blandishments could touch his convictions of duty.

And when the advocates of slavery turned upon him with anger and menace, he hurled at them with prouder defiance his answer, repeating itself in endless variations: "You must yield, for you are wrong."

The slave power had so frequently succeeded in making the North yield to its demands, even after the most formidable demonstrations of reluctance, that it had become a serious question whether there existed any such thing as Northern firmness. But it did exist, and in Charles Sumner it had developed its severest political type. The stronger the assault, the higher rose in him the power of resistance. In him lived that spirit which not only would not yield, but would turn upon the assailant. The Southern force, which believed itself irresistible, found itself striking against a body which was immovable. To think of yielding to any demand of slavery, of making a compromise with it, in however tempting a form, was, to his nature, an absolute impossibility.

Mr. Sumner's courage was of a peculiar kind. He attacked the slave power in the most unsparing manner, when its supporters were most violent in resenting opposition, and when that violence was always apt to proceed from words to blows. One day, while Sumner was delivering one of his severest speeches, Stephen A. Douglass, walking up and down behind the President's chair in the old Senate-chamber, and listening to him, remarked to a friend: "Do you hear that man? He may be a fool, but I tell you that man has pluck. I wonder whether he knows himself what he is doing. I am not sure whether I should have the courage to say those things to the men who are scowling around him."

Of all men in the Senate-chamber, Sumner was probably least aware that the thing he did required pluck. He simply did what he felt it his duty to his cause to do. It was to him a matter of course. He was like a soldier who, when he has to march upon the enemy's batteries, does not say to himself: "Now I am going to perform an act of heroism," but who simply obeys an impulse of duty, and marches forward without thinking of the bullets that fly around his head. A thought of the boldness of what he has done may then occur to him afterwards, when he is told of it. This was one of the striking peculiarities of Mr. Sumner's character, as all those know who knew him well.

Neither was he conscious of the stinging force of the language he frequently employed. He simply uttered, what he felt to be true, in language fitting the strength of his convictions. The indignation of his moral sense at what he felt to be wrong was so deep and sincere that he thought everybody must find the extreme severity of his expressions as natural as they came to his own mind. And he was not unfrequently surprised, greatly surprised, when others found his language offensive.

As he possessed the firmness and courage, so he possessed the faith of the devotee. From the beginning, and through all the vicissitudes of the anti-slavery movement, his heart was profoundly assured that his generation would see slavery entirely extinguished.

While travelling in France to restore his health, after having been beaten down on the floor of the Senate, he visited Alexis de Tocqueville, the celebrated author of "Democracy in America." Tocqueville expressed his anxiety about the issue of the anti-slavery movement, which then had suffered defeat by the election of Buchanan. "There can be no doubt about the result," said Sumner. "Slavery will soon succumb and disappear." "Disappear! in what way, and how soon?" asked Tocqueville. "In what manner I cannot say," replied Sumner. "How soon I cannot say. But it will be soon; I feel it; I know it. It cannot be otherwise." That was all the reason he gave. "Mr. Sumner is a remarkable man," said de Tocqueville afterwards to a friend of mine. "He says that slavery will soon entirely disappear in the United States. He does not know how, he does not know when, but he feels it, he is perfectly sure of it. The man speaks like a prophet." And so it was.

What appeared a perplexing puzzle to other men's minds was perfectly clear to him. His method of reasoning was simple; it was the reasoning of religious faith. Slavery is wrong,— therefore it must and will perish; freedom is right,— therefore it must and will prevail. And by no power of resistance, by no difficulty, by no disappointment, by no defeat, could that faith be shaken. For his cause, so great and just, he thought nothing impossible, everything certain. And he was unable to understand how others could fail to share his faith.

In one sense he was no party leader. He possessed none of the instinct or experience of the politician, nor that sagacity of mind which appreciates and measures the importance of changing circumstances, or the possibilities and opportunities of the day. He lacked, entirely, the genius of organization. He never understood, nor did he value, the art of strengthening his following by timely concession, or prudent reticence, or advantageous combination and alliance. He knew nothing of management and party manœuvre. Indeed, not unfrequently he alarmed many devoted friends of his cause by bold declarations, for which, they thought, the public mind was not prepared, and by the unreserved avowal and straightforward advocacy of ultimate objects, which, they thought, might safely be left to the natural development of events. He was not seldom accused of doing things calculated to frighten the people and to disorganize the anti-slavery forces.

Such was his unequivocal declaration in his first great anti-slavery speech in the Senate, that he held himself bound by every conviction of justice, right and duty, to disobey the fugitive slave law, and his ringing answer to the question put by Senator Butler of South Carolina, whether, without the fugitive slave law, he would, under the Constitution, consider it his duty to aid the surrender of fugitive slaves, "Is thy servant a dog, that he should do this thing?"

Such was his speech on the "Barbarism of Slavery," delivered on a bill to admit Kansas immediately under a free State Constitution; a speech so unsparing and vehement in the denunciation of slavery in all its political, moral and social aspects, and so direct in its prediction of the complete annihilation of slavery, that it was said such a speech would scarcely aid the admission of Kansas.

Such was his unbending and open resistance to any plan of compromise calculated to preserve slavery, when upon Mr. Lincoln's election, the Rebellion first raised its head, and a large number of Northern people, even anti-slavery men, frightened by the threatening prospect of civil war, cast blindly about for a plan of adjustment, while really no adjustment was possible.

Such was, early in the war, and during its most doubtful hours, his declaration, laid before the Senate in a series of resolutions, that the States in rebellion had destroyed themselves as such by the very act of rebellion; that slavery, as a creation of State law, had perished with the States, and that general emancipation must immediately follow, — thus putting the programme of emancipation boldly in the foreground, at a time when many thought that the cry of union alone, union with or without slavery, could hold together the Union forces.

Such was his declaration, demanding negro suffrage even before the close of the war, while the public opinion at the North, whose aid the government needed, still recoiled from such a measure.

Thus he was apt to go rough-shod over the considerations of management, deemed important by his co-workers. I believe he never consulted with his friends around him, before doing those things, and when they afterwards remonstrated with him, he ingenuously asked: " Is it not right and true, what I have said? And if it is right and true, must I not say it?"

And yet, although he had no organizing mind, and despised management, he was a leader. He was a leader, as the embodiment of the moral idea, with all its uncompromising firmness, its unflagging faith, its daring devotion. And in this sense he could be a leader only because he was no politician. He forced others to follow, because he was himself impracticable. Simply obeying his moral impulse, he dared to say things which in the highest legislative body of the Republic nobody else would say; and he proved that they could be said, and yet the world would move on. With his wealth of learning and his legal ability, he furnished an arsenal of arguments, convincing more timid souls that what he said could be sustained in repeating. And presently the politicians felt encouraged to follow in the direction where the idealist had driven a stake ahead. Nay, he forced them to follow, for they knew that the idealist, whom they could not venture to disown, would not fall back at their bidding. Such was his leadership in the struggle with slavery.

Nor was that leadership interrupted when, on the 22d of May, 1856, Preston Brooks of South Carolina, maddened by an arraignment of his State and its Senator, came upon Charles Sumner in the Senate, struck him down with heavy blows and left him on the ground bleeding and insensible. For three years Sumner's voice was not heard, but his blood marked the vantage ground from which his party could not recede; and his senatorial chair, kept empty for him by the noble people of Massachusetts, stood there in most eloquent silence, confirming, sealing, inflaming all he had said with terrible illustration,— a guide-post to the onward march of freedom.

When, in 1861, the Republican party had taken the reins of government in hand, his peculiar leadership entered upon a new field of action. No sooner was the victory of the anti-slavery cause in the election ascertained, than the Rebellion raised its head. South Carolina opened the secession movement. The portentous shadow of an approaching civil war spread over the land. A tremor fluttered through the hearts even of strong men in the North, — a vague fear such as is produced by the first rumbling of an earthquake. Could not a bloody conflict be averted? A fresh clamor for compromise arose. Even Republicans in Congress began to waver. The proposed compromise involved new and express constitutional recognitions of the existence and rights of slavery, and guarantees against interference with it by constitutional amendment or national law. The pressure from the country, even from Massachusetts, in favor of the scheme, was extraordinary, but a majority of the anti-slavery men in the Senate, in their front Mr. Sumner, stood firm, feeling that a compromise, giving express constitutional sanction and an indefinite lease of life to slavery, would be a surrender, and knowing, also, that even by the offer of such a surrender, secession and civil war would still be insisted on by the Southern leaders. The history of those days, as we now know it, confirms the accuracy of that judgment. The war was inevitable. Thus the anti-slavery cause escaped a useless humiliation, and retained intact its moral force for future action.

But now the time had come when the anti-slavery movement, no longer a mere opposition to the demands of the slave power, was to proceed to positive action. The war had scarcely commenced in earnest, when Mr. Sumner urged general emancipation. Only the great ideal object of the liberty of all men could give sanction to a war in the eyes of the devotee of universal peace. To the end of stamping upon the war the character of a war of emancipation all his energies were bent. His unreserved and emphatic utterances alarmed the politicians. Our armies suffered disaster upon disaster in the field. The managing mind insisted that care must be taken, by nourishing the popular enthusiasm for the integrity of the Union, — the strictly national idea alone, — to unite all the social and political elements of the North for the struggle; and that so bold a measure as immediate emancipation might reanimate old dissensions, and put hearty co-operation in jeopardy.

But Mr. Sumner's convictions could not be repressed. In a bold decree of universal liberty he saw only a new source of inspiration and strength. Nor was his impulsive instinct unsupported by good reason. The distraction produced in the North by an emancipation measure could only be of short duration. The moral spirit was certain, ultimately, to gain the upper hand.

But in another direction a bold and unequivocal anti-slavery policy could not fail to produce most salutary effects. One of the dangers threatening us was foreign interference. No European powers gave us their expressed sympathy except Germany and Russia. The governing classes of England, with conspicuous individual exceptions, always gratefully to be remembered, were ill-disposed towards the Union cause. The permanent disruption of the Republic was loudly predicted, as if it were desired, and intervention — an intervention which could be only in favor of the South — was openly spoken of. The Emperor of the French, who availed himself of our embarrassments to execute his ambitious designs in Mexico, was animated by sentiments no less hostile. It appeared as if only a plausible opportunity had been wanting, to bring foreign intervention upon our heads. A threatening spirit, disarmed only by timely prudence, had manifested itself in the Trent case. It seemed doubtful whether the most skilful diplomacy, unaided by a stronger force, would be able to avert the danger.

But the greatest strength of the anti-slavery cause had always been in the conscience of mankind. There was our natural ally. The cause of slavery as such could have no open sympathy among the nations of Europe. It stood condemned by the moral sentiment of the civilized world. How could any European government, in the face of that universal sentiment, undertake openly to interfere against a power waging war against slavery? Surely, that could not be thought of.

But had the government of the United States distinctly professed that it was waging war against slavery, and for freedom? Had it not been officially declared that the war for the Union would not alter the condition of a single human being in America? Why then not arrest the useless effusion of blood; why not, by intervention, stop a destructive war, in which, confessedly, slavery and freedom were not at stake? Such were the arguments of our enemies in Europe; and they were not without color.

It was obvious that nothing but a measure impressing beyond dispute upon our war a decided anti-slavery character, making it in profession what it was inevitably destined to be in fact, a war of emancipation, — could enlist on our side the enlightened public opinion of the Old

World so strongly as to restrain the hostile spirit of foreign governments. No European government could well venture to interfere against those who had convinced the world that they were fighting to give freedom to the slaves of North America.

Thus the moral instinct did not err. The emancipation policy was not only the policy of principle, but also the policy of safety. Mr. Sumner urged it with impetuous and unflagging zeal. In the Senate he found but little encouragement. The resolutions he introduced in February, 1862, declaring State suicide as the consequence of Rebellion, and the extinction of slavery in the insurrectionary States as the consequence of State suicide, were looked upon as an ill-timed and hazardous demonstration, disturbing all ideas of management.

To the President, then, he devoted his efforts. Nothing could be more interesting, nay, touching, than the peculiar relations that sprung up between Abraham Lincoln and Charles Sumner. No two men could be more alike as to their moral impulses and ultimate aims; no two men more unlike in their methods of reasoning and their judgment of means.

Abraham Lincoln was a true child of the people. There was in his heart an inexhaustible fountain of tenderness, and from it sprung that longing to be true, just and merciful to all, which made the people love him. In the deep, large humanity of his soul had grown his moral and political principles, to which he clung with the fidelity of an honest nature, and which he defended with the strength of a vigorous mind.

But he had not grown great in any high school of

statesmanship. He had, from the humblest beginnings, slowly and laboriously worked himself up, or rather he had gradually risen up without being aware of it, and suddenly he found himself in the foremost rank of the distinguished men of the land. In his youth and early manhood he had achieved no striking successes that might have imparted to him that overweening self-appreciation which so frequently leads self-made men to overestimate their faculties, and to ignore the limits of their strength. He was not a learned man, but he had learned and meditated enough to feel how much there was still for him to learn. His marvellous success in his riper years left intact the inborn modesty of his nature. He was absolutely without pretension. His simplicity, which by its genuineness extorted respect and affection, was wonderfully persuasive, and sometimes deeply pathetic and strikingly brilliant.

His natural gifts were great; he possessed a clear and penetrating mind, but in forming his opinions on subjects of importance, he was so careful, conscientious and diffident, that he would always hear and probe what opponents had to say, before he became firmly satisfied of the justness of his own conclusions, — not as if he had been easily controlled and led by other men, for he had a will of his own; — but his mental operations were slow and hesitating, and inapt to conceive quick resolutions. He lacked self-reliance. Nobody felt more than he the awful weight of his responsibilities. He was not one of those bold reformers who will defy the opposition of the world and undertake to impose their opinions and will upon a reluctant age. With careful consideration of the possibilities of the hour he advanced slowly, but when he had so advanced, he planted his foot with firmness, and no power was strong enough to force him to a backward step. And every day of great responsibility enlarged the horizon of his mind, and every day he grasped the helm of affairs with a steadier hand.

It was to such a man that Sumner, during the most doubtful days at the beginning of the war, addressed his appeals for immediate emancipation, — appeals impetuous and impatient as they could spring only from his ardent and overruling convictions.

The President at first passively resisted the vehement counsel of the Senator, but he bade the counsellor welcome. It was Mr. Lincoln's constant endeavor to surround himself with the best and ablest men of the country. Not only did the first names of the Republican party appear in his cabinet, but every able man in Congress was always invited as an adviser, whether his views agreed with those of the President or not. But Mr. Sumner he treated as a favorite counsellor, almost like a Minister of State, outside of the cabinet.

There were statesmen around the President who were also politicians, understanding the art of management. Mr. Lincoln appreciated the value of their advice as to what was prudent and practicable. But he knew also how to discriminate. In Mr. Sumner he saw a counsellor who was no politician, but who stood before him as the true representative of the moral earnestness, of the great inspirations of their common cause. From him he heard what was right, and necessary, and inevitable. By the former he was told what, in their opinion, could prudently and safely be done. Having heard them both, Abraham Lincoln counselled with himself, and formed his resolution. Thus Mr. Lincoln, while scarcely ever fully and speedily following Sumner's advice, never ceased to ask for it, for he knew its significance. And Sumner, while almost always dissatisfied with Lincoln's cautious hesitation, never grew weary in giving his advice, for he never distrusted Lincoln's fidelity. Always agreed as to the ultimate end, they almost always differed as to times and means; but, while differing, they firmly trusted, for they understood one another.

And thus their mutual respect grew into an affectionate friendship, which no clash of disagreeing opinions could break. Sumner loved to tell his friends, after Lincoln's death, — and I heard him relate it often, never without an expression of tenderness, — how at one time those who disliked and feared his intimacy with the President, and desired to see it disrupted, thought it was irreparably broken. It was at the close of Lincoln's first administration, in 1865, when the President had proposed certain measures of reconstruction, touching the State of Louisiana.

The end of the session of Congress was near at hand, and the success of the bill depended on a vote of the Senate before the hour of adjournment on the 4th of March. Mr. Lincoln had the measure very much at heart. But Sumner opposed it, because it did not contain sufficient guarantees for the rights of the colored people, and by a parliamentary manœuvre, simply consuming time until the adjournment came, he with two or three other Senators succeeded in defeating it. Lincoln was reported to be deeply chagrined at Sumner's action, and the newspapers already announced that the breach between Lincoln and Sumner was complete, and could not be healed. But those who said so did not know the men. On the night of the 6th of March, two days after Lincoln's second inauguration, the customary inauguration ball was to take place. Sumner did not think of attending it. But towards evening he received a card from the President, which read thus: "Dear Mr. Sumner, unless you send me word to the contrary, I shall this evening call with my carriage at your house, to take you with me to the inauguration ball. Sincerely yours, ABRAHAM LINCOLN." Mr. Sumner, deeply touched, at once made up his mind to go to an inauguration ball for the first time. Soon the carriage arrived, the President invited Sumner to take a seat in it with him, and Sumner found there Mrs. Lincoln and Mr. Colfax, the Speaker of the House of Representatives. Arrived at the ball-room, the President asked Mr. Sumner to offer his arm to Mrs. Lincoln; and the astonished spectators, who had been made to believe that the breach between Lincoln and Sumner was irreparable, beheld the President's wife on the arm of the Senator, and the Senator, on that occasion of State, invited to take the seat of honor by the President's side. Not a word passed between them about their disagreement.

The world became convinced that such a friendship between such men could not be broken by a mere honest difference of opinion. Abraham Lincoln, a man of sincere and profound convictions himself, esteemed and honored sincere and profound convictions in others. It was thus that Abraham Lincoln composed his quarrels with his friends, and at his bedside, when he died, there was no mourner more deeply afflicted than Charles Sumner.

Let me return to the year 1862. Long, incessant and arduous was Sumner's labor for emancipation. At last the great Proclamation, which sealed the fate of slavery, came, and no man had done more to bring it forth than he.

Still, Charles Sumner thought his work far from accomplished. During the three years of war that followed, so full of vicissitudes, alarms and anxieties, he stood in the Senate and in the President's closet as the ever-watchful sentinel of freedom and equal rights. No occasion eluded his grasp to push on the destruction of slavery, not only by sweeping decrees, but in detail, by pursuing it, as with a probing-iron, into every nook and corner of its existence. It was his sleepless care that every blow struck at the Rebellion should surely and heavily tell against slavery, and that every drop of American blood that was shed should surely be consecrated to human freedom. He could not rest until assurance was made doubly sure, and I doubt whether our legislative history shows an example of equal watchfulness, fidelity and devotion to a great object. Such was the character of Mr. Sumner's legislative activity during the war.

As the Rebellion succumbed, new problems arose. To set upon their feet again States disorganized by insurrection and civil war; to remodel a society which had been lifted out of its ancient hinges by the sudden change of its system of labor; to protect the emancipated slaves against the old pretension of absolute control on the part of their former masters; to guard society against the possible transgressions of a large multitude long held in slavery and ignorance and now suddenly set free; so to lodge political power in this inflammable state of things as to prevent violent reactions and hostile collisions; to lead social forces so discordant into orderly and fruitful co-operation, and to infuse into communities, but recently rent by the most violent passions, a new spirit of loyal attachment to a common nationality,— this was certainly one of the most perplexing tasks ever imposed upon the statesmanship of any time and any country.

But to Mr. Sumner's mind the problem of reconstruction did not appear perplexing at all. Believing, as he always did, that the Democratic idea, as he found it defined in the Declaration of Independence, "Human rights in their utmost expansion," contained an ultimately certain solution of all difficulties, he saw the principal aim to be reached by any reconstruction policy, in the investment of the emancipated slaves with all the rights and privileges of American citizenship. The complexity of the problem, the hazardous character of the experiment, never troubled him. And as, early in the war, he had for himself laid down the theory that, by the very act of rebellion, the insurrectionary States had destroyed themselves as such, so he argued now, with assured consistency, that those States had relapsed into a territorial condition; that the national government had to fill the void by creations of its own, and that in doing so the establishment of universal suffrage there was an unavoidable necessity. Thus he marched forward to the realization of his ideal, on the straightest line, and with the firmness of profound conviction.

In the discussions which followed, he had the advantage

of a man who knows exactly what he wants, and who is imperturbably, religiously convinced that he is right. But his constitutional theory, as well as the measures he proposed, found little favor in Congress. The public mind struggled long against the results he had pointed out as inevitable. The whole power of President Johnson's administration was employed to lead the development of things in another direction. But through all the vacillations of public opinion, through all the perplexities in which Congress entangled itself, the very necessity of things seemed to press toward the ends which Sumner and those who thought like him had advocated from the beginning.

At last, Mr. Sumner saw the fondest dreams of his life soon realized. Slavery was forever blotted out in this Republic by the 13th Amendment to the Constitution. By the 14th the emancipated slaves were secured in their rights of citizenship before the law, and the 15th guaranteed to them the right to vote.

It was, indeed, a most astonishing, a marvellous consummation. What ten years before not even the most sanguine would have ventured to anticipate, what only the profound faith of the devotee could believe possible, was done. And no man had a better right than Charles Sumner to claim for himself a pre-eminent share in that great consummation. He had, indeed, not been the originator of most of the practical measures of legislation by which such results were reached. He had even combated some of them as in conflict with his theories. He did not possess the peculiar ability of constructing policies in detail, of taking account of existing circumstances and advantage of opportunities. But he had resolutely marched ahead of public opinion in marking the ends to be reached. Nobody had done more to inspire and strengthen the moral spirit of the anti-slavery cause. He stood foremost among the propelling, driving forces which pushed on the great work with undaunted courage, untiring effort, irresistible energy and religious devotion. No man's singleness of purpose, fidelity and faith surpassed his, and when by future generations the names are called which are inseparably united with the deliverance of the American Republic from slavery, no name will be called before his own.

While the championship of human rights is his first title to fame, I should be unjust to his merit, did I omit to mention the services he rendered on another field of action. When, in 1861, the secession of the Southern States left the anti-slavery party in the majority in the Senate of the United States, Charles Sumner was placed as chairman at the head of the Committee on Foreign Relations. It was a high distinction, and no selection could have been more fortunate. Without belittling others, it may be said that of the many able men then and since in the Senate, Mr. Sumner was by far the fittest for that responsible position. He had ever since his college days made international law a special and favorite study, and was perfectly familiar with its principles, the history of its development, and its literature. Nothing of importance had ever been published on that subject in any language that had escaped his attention. His knowledge of history was uncommonly extensive and accurate; all the leading international law cases, with their incidents in detail, their theories and settlements, he had at his fingers' ends ; and to his last day he remained indefatigable in inquiry. Moreover, he had seen the world ; he had studied the institutions and policies of foreign countries, on their own soil, aided by his personal intercourse with many of their leading statesmen, not a few of whom remained in friendly correspondence with him ever since their first acquaintance.

No public man had a higher appreciation of the position, dignity, and interests of his own country, and no one was less liable than he to be carried away or driven to hasty and ill-considered steps, by excited popular clamor. He was ever strenuous in asserting our own rights, while his sense of justice did not permit him to be regardless of the rights of other nations. His abhorrence of the barbarities of war, and his ardent love of peace, led him earnestly to seek for every international difference a peaceable solution ; and where no settlement could be reached by the direct negotiations of diplomacy, the idea of arbitration was always uppermost in his mind. He desired to raise the Republic to the high office of a missionary of peace and civilization in the world. He was, therefore, not only an uncommonly well-informed, enlightened and experienced, but also an eminently conservative, cautious and safe counsellor ; and the few instances in which he appeared more impulsive than prudent will, upon candid investigation, not impugn this statement. I am far from claiming for him absolute correctness of view, and infallibility of judgment in every case ; but taking his whole career together, it may well be doubted, whether in the whole history of the Republic, the Senate of the United States ever possessed a chairman of the Committee on

Foreign Relations who united in himself, in such completeness, the qualifications necessary and desirable for the important and delicate duties of that position. This may sound like the extravagant praise of a personal friend; but it is the sober opinion of men most competent to judge, that it does not go beyond his merits.

His qualities were soon put to the test. Early in the war one of the gallant captains of our navy arrested the British mail steamer Trent, running from one neutral port to another, on the high seas, and took from her by force Mason and Slidell, two emissaries of the Confederate Government, and their despatches. The people of the North loudly applauded the act. The Secretary of the Navy approved it. The House of Representatives commended it in resolutions. Even in the Senate a majority seemed inclined to stand by it. The British Government, in a threatening tone, demanded the instant restitution of the prisoners, and an apology. The people of the North responded with a shout of indignation at British insolence. The excitement seemed irrepressible. Those in quest of popularity saw a chance to win it easily by bellicose declamation.

But among those who felt the weight of responsibility more moderate counsels prevailed. The Government wisely resolved to surrender the prisoners, and peace with Great Britain was preserved.

It was Mr. Sumner who threw himself into the breach against the violent drift of public opinion. In a speech in the Senate, no less remarkable for patriotic spirit than legal learning and ingenious and irresistible argument, he justified the surrender of the prisoners, not on the ground that during our struggle with the Rebellion we were not in a condition to go to war with Great Britain, but on the higher ground that the surrender, demanded by Great Britain in violation of her own traditional pretensions as to the rights of belligerents, was in perfect accord with American precedent, and the advanced principles of our government concerning the rights of neutrals, and that this very act, therefore, would for all time constitute an additional and most conspicuous precedent to aid in the establishment of more humane rules for the protection of the rights of neutrals and the mitigation of the injustice and barbarity attending maritime war.

The success of this argument was complete. It turned the tide of public opinion. It convinced the American people that this was not an act of pusillanimity, but of justice; not a humiliation of the Republic, but a noble vindication of her time-honored principles, and a service rendered to the cause of progress.

Other complications followed. The interference of European powers in Mexico came. Excited demands for intervention on our part were made in the Senate, and Mr. Sumner, trusting that the victory of the Union over the Rebellion would bring on the deliverance of Mexico in its train, with signal moderation and tact prevented the agitation of so dangerous a policy. It is needless to mention the many subsequent instances in which his wisdom and skill rendered the Republic similar service.

Only one of his acts provoked comment in foreign countries calculated to impair the high esteem in which his name was universally held there. It was his speech on the Alabama case, preceding the rejection by the

Senate of the Clarendon-Johnson treaty. He was accused of having yielded to a vulgar impulse of demagogism in flattering and exciting, by unfair statements and extravagant demands, the grudge the American people might bear to England. No accusation could possibly be more unjust, and I know whereof I speak. Mr. Sumner loved England — had loved her as long as he lived — from a feeling of consanguinity, for the treasures of literature she had given to the world, for the services she had rendered to human freedom, for the blows she had struck at slavery, for the sturdy work she had done for the cause of progress and civilization, for the many dear friends he had among her citizens. Such was his impulse, and no man was more incapable of pandering to a vulgar prejudice.

I will not deny that as to our differences with Great Britain he was not entirely free from personal feeling. That the England he loved so well — the England of Clarkson and Wilberforce, of Cobden and Bright; the England to whom he had looked as the champion of the anti-slavery cause in the world — should make such hot haste to recognize, nay, as he termed it, to set up, on the seas, as a belligerent, that Rebellion, whose avowed object it was to found an empire of slavery, and to aid that Rebellion by every means short of open war against the Union,— that was a shock to his feelings which he felt like a betrayal of friendship. And yet while that feeling appeared in the warmth of his language, it did not dictate his policy. I will not discuss here the correctness of his opinions as to what he styled the precipitate and unjustifiable recognition of Southern belligerency, or his theory of consequential damages. What he desired to accomplish was, not to extort from England a large sum of money, but to put our grievance in the strongest light; to convince England of the great wrong she had inflicted upon us, and thus to prepare a composition, which, consisting more in the settlement of great principles and rules of international law to govern the future intercourse of nations, than in the payment of large damages, would remove all questions of difference, and serve to restore and confirm a friendship which ought never to have been interrupted.

When, finally, the Treaty of Washington was negotiated by the Joint High Commission, Mr. Sumner, although thinking that more might have been accomplished, did not only not oppose that treaty, but actively aided in securing for it the consent of the Senate. Nothing would have been more painful to him than a continuance of unfriendly relations with Great Britain. Had there been danger of war, no man's voice would have pleaded with more fervor to avert such a calamity. He gave ample proof that he did not desire any personal opinions to stand in the way of a settlement, and if that settlement, which he willingly supported, did not in every respect satisfy him, it was because he desired to put the future relations of the two countries upon a still safer and more enduring basis.

No statesman ever took part in the direction of our foreign affairs who so completely identified himself with the most advanced, humane and progressive principles. Ever jealous of the honor of his country, he sought to elevate that honor by a policy scrupulously just to the strong, and generous to the weak. A profound lover of peace, he faithfully advocated arbitration as a substitute for war. The barbarities of war he constantly labored to mitigate. In the hottest days of our civil conflict he protested against the issue of letters of marque and reprisal; he never lost an opportunity to condemn privateering as a barbarous practice, and he even went so far as to designate the system of prize-money as inconsistent with our enlightened civilization. In some respects, his principles were in advance of our time; but surely the day will come when this Republic, marching in the front of progress, will adopt them as her own, and remember their champion with pride.

I now approach the last period of his life, which brought to him new and bitter struggles.

The work of reconstruction completed, he felt that three objects still demanded new efforts. One was that the colored race should be protected by national legislation against degrading discrimination, in the enjoyment of facilities of education, travel and pleasure, such as stand under the control of law; and this object he embodied in his civil-rights bill, of which he was the mover and especial champion. The second was, that generous reconciliation should wipe out the lingering animosities of past conflicts and reunite in new bonds of brotherhood all those who had been divided. And the third was, that the government should be restored to the purity and high tone of its earlier days, and that from its new birth the republic should issue with a new lustre of moral greatness, to lead its children to a higher perfection of manhood, and to be a shining example and beacon-light to all the nations of the earth.

This accomplished, he often said to his friends he would be content to lie down and die; but death overtook him before he was thus content, and before death came he was destined to taste more of the bitterness of life.

His civil-rights bill he pressed with unflagging perseverance, against an opposition which stood upon the ground that the objects his measure contemplated, belonged, under the Constitution, to the jurisdiction of the States; that the colored people, armed with the ballot, possessed the necessary means to provide for their own security, and that the progressive development of public sentiment would afford to them greater protection than could be given by national legislation of questionable constitutionality.

The pursuit of the other objects brought upon him experiences of a painful nature. I have to speak of his disagreement with the administration of President Grant and with his party. Nothing could be farther from my desire than to reopen, on a solemn occasion like this, those bitter conflicts which are still so fresh in our minds, and to assail any living man in the name of the dead. Were it my purpose to attack, I should do so in my own name and choose the place where I can be answered, — not this. But I have a duty to perform; it is to set forth in the light of truth the motives of the dead before the living. I knew Charles Sumner's motives well. We stood together shoulder to shoulder in many a hard contest. We were friends, and between us passed those confidences which only intimate friendship knows. Therefore I can truly say that I knew his motives well.

The civil war had greatly changed the country, and left many problems behind it, requiring again that building, organizing, constructive kind of statesmanship which I described as presiding over the Republic in its earlier history. For a solution of many of those problems Mr. Sumner's mind was little fitted, and he naturally turned to those which appealed to his moral nature. No great civil war has ever passed over any country, especially a republic, without producing wide-spread and dangerous demoralization and corruption, not only in the government, but among the people. In such times the sordid instincts of human nature develop themselves to unusual recklessness under the guise of patriotism. The ascendancy of no political party in a republic has ever been long maintained without tempting many of its members to avail themselves for their selfish advantage of the opportunities of power and party protection, and without attracting a horde of camp followers, professing principle, but meaning spoil. It has always been so, and the American Republic has not escaped the experience.

Neither Mr. Sumner nor many others could in our circumstances close their eyes to this fact. He recognized the danger early, and already, in 1864, he introduced in the Senate a bill for the reform of the civil service, crude in its detail, but embodying correct principles. Thus he may be said to have been the earliest pioneer of the Civil Service Reform movement.

The evil grew under President Johnson's administration, and ever since it has been cropping out, not only drawn to light by the efforts of the opposition, but voluntarily and involuntarily, by members of the ruling party itself. There were in it many men who confessed to themselves the urgent necessity of meeting the growing danger.

Mr. Sumner could not be silent. He cherished in his mind a high ideal of what this Republic and its government should be: a government composed of the best and wisest of the land; animated by none but the highest and most patriotic aspirations; yielding to no selfish impulse; noble in its tone and character; setting its face sternly against all wrong and injustice; presenting in its whole being to the American people a shining example of purity and lofty public spirit. Mr. Sumner was proud of his country; there was no prouder American in the land. He felt in himself the whole dignity of the Republic. And when he saw anything that lowered the dignity of the Republic and the character of its government, he felt it as he would have felt a personal offence. He criticised it, he denounced it, he remonstrated against it, for he could not do otherwise. He did so, frequently and without hesitation and reserve, when Mr. Lincoln was President. He continued to do so ever since, the more loudly, the more difficult it was to make himself heard. It was his nature; he felt it to be his right as a citizen; he esteemed it his duty as a Senator.

That, and no other, was the motive which impelled him. The rupture with the administration was brought on by his opposition to the Santo Domingo Treaty. In the reasons upon which that opposition was based, I know that personal feeling had no share. They were patriotic reasons, publicly and candidly expressed, and it seems they were appreciated by a very large portion of the American people. It has been said that he provoked the resentment of the President by first promising to support that treaty and then opposing it, thus rendering himself guilty of an act of duplicity. He has publicly denied the justice of the charge and stated the facts as they stood in his memory. I am willing to make the fullest allowance for the possibility of a misapprehension of words. But I affirm, also, that no living man who knew Mr. Sumner well, will hesitate a moment to pronounce the charge of duplicity as founded on the most radical of misapprehensions. An act of duplicity on his part was simply a moral impossibility. It was absolutely foreign to his nature. Whatever may have been the defects of his character, he never knowingly deceived a human being. There was in him not the faintest shadow of dissimulation, disguise or trickery. Not one of his words ever had the purpose of a double meaning, not one of his acts a hidden aim. His likes and dislikes, his approval and disapproval, as soon as they were clear to his own consciousness, appeared before the world in the open light of noonday. His frankness was so unbounded, his candor so entire, his ingenuousness so childlike, that he lacked even the discretion of ordinary prudence. He was almost incapable of moderating his feelings, of toning down his meaning in the expression. When he might have gained a point by indirection, he would not have done so, because he could not. He was one of those who, when they attack, attack always in front and in broad daylight. The night surprise and the flank march were absolutely foreign to his tactics, because they were incompatible with his nature. I have known many men in my life, but never one who was less capable of a perfidious act or an artful profession.

Call him a vain, an impracticable, an imperious man, if you will, but American history does not mention the name of one, of whom with greater justice it can be said that he was a true man.

The same candor and purity of motives which prompted and characterized his opposition to the Santo Domingo scheme, prompted and characterized the attacks upon the administration which followed. The charges he made, and the arguments with which he supported them, I feel not called upon to enumerate. Whether and how far they were correct or erroneous, just or unjust, important or unimportant, the judgment of history will determine. May that judgment be just and fair to us all. But this I can affirm to-day, for I know it: Charles Sumner never made a charge which he did not himself firmly, religiously believe to be true. Neither did he condemn those he attacked for anything he did not firmly, religiously believe to be wrong. And while attacking those in power for what he considered wrong, he was always ready to support them in all he considered right. After all he has said of the President, he would to-day, if he lived, conscientiously, cordially, joyously aid in sustaining the President's recent veto on an act of financial legislation which threatened to inflict a deep injury on the character, as well as the true interests of the American people.

But at the time of which I speak, all he said was so deeply grounded in his feeling and conscience, that it was for him difficult to understand how others could form different conclusions. When, shortly before the National Republican Convention of 1872, he had delivered in the Senate that fierce philippic for which he has been censured so much, he turned to me with the question, whether I did not think that the statements and arguments he had produced would certainly exercise a decisive influence on the action of that convention. I replied that I thought it would not. He was greatly astonished, — not as if he indulged in the delusion that his personal word would have such authoritative weight, but it seemed impossible to him that opinions which in him had risen to the full strength of overruling conviction, that a feeling of duty which in him had grown so solemn and irresistible as to inspire him to any risk and sacrifice, ever so painful, should fall powerless at the feet of a party which so long had followed inspirations kindred to his own. Such was the ingenuousness of his nature; such his faith in the rectitude of his own cause. The result of his effort is a matter of history. After the Philadelphia convention, and not until then, he resolved to oppose his party, and to join a movement which was doomed to defeat. He obeyed his sense of right and duty at a terrible sacrifice.

He had been one of the great chiefs of his party, by many regarded as the greatest. He had stood in the Senate as a mighty monument of the struggles and victories of the anti-slavery cause. He had been a martyr of his earnestness. By all Republicans he had been looked up to with respect, by many with veneration. He had been the idol of the people of his State. All this was suddenly changed. Already, at the time of his opposition to the Santo Domingo scheme, he had been deprived of his place at the head of the Senate Committee on Foreign Relations, which he had held so long, and with so much honor to the republic and to himself. But few know how sharp a pang it gave to his heart, this removal, which he felt as the wanton degradation of a faithful servant who was conscious of only doing his duty.

But, when he had pronounced against the candidates of his party, worse experiences were for him in store. Journals which for years had been full of his praise now assailed him with remorseless ridicule and vituperation, questioning even his past services and calling him a traitor. Men who had been proud of his acquaintance turned away their heads when they met him in the street. Former flatterers eagerly covered his name with slander. Many of those who had been his associates in the struggle for freedom sullenly withdrew from him their friendship. Even some men of the colored race, for whose elevation he had labored with a fidelity and devotion equalled by few and surpassed by none, joined in the chorus of denunciation. Oh, how keenly he felt it! And, as if the cruel malice of ingratitude and the unsparing persecution of infuriated partisanship had not been enough, another enemy came upon him, threatening his very life. It was a new attack of that disease which, for many years, from time to time, had prostrated him with the acutest suffering, and which shortly should lay him low. It admonished him that every word he spoke might be his last. He found himself forced to leave the field of a contest in which not only his principles of right, but even his good name, earned by so many years of faithful effort, was at stake. He possessed no longer the elastic spirit of youth, and the prospect of new struggles had ceased to charm him. His hair had grown gray with years, and he had reached that age when a statesman begins to love the thought of reposing his head upon the pillow of assured public esteem. Even the sweet comfort of that sanctuary was denied him, in which the voice of wife and child would have said: Rest here, for whatever the world may say, we know that you are good and faithful and noble. Only the friends of his youth, who knew him best, surrounded him with never-flagging confidence and love, and those of his companions-in-arms, who knew him also, and who were true to him as they were true to their common cause. Thus he stood in the presidential campaign of 1872.

It is at such a moment of bitter ordeal that an honest public man feels the impulse of retiring within himself; to examine with scrupulous care the quality of his own motives; anxiously to inquire whether he is really right in his opinions and objects when so many old friends say that he is wrong; and then, after such a review at the hand of conscience and duty, to form anew his conclusions without bias, and to proclaim them without fear. This he did.

He had desired, and as he wrote, "he had confidently hoped, on returning home from Washington, to meet his fellow-citizens in Faneuil Hall, that venerable forum, and to speak once more on great questions involving the welfare of the country, but recurring symptoms of a painful character warned him against such an attempt." The speech he had intended to pronounce, but could not, he left in a written form for publication, and went to Europe, seeking rest, uncertain whether he would ever return alive. In it he reiterated all the reasons which had forced him to oppose the administration and the candidates of his party. They were unchanged. Then followed an earnest and pathetic plea for universal peace and reconciliation. He showed how necessary the revival of fraternal feeling was, not only for the prosperity and physical well-being, but for the moral elevation of the American people and for the safety and greatness of the Republic. He gave words to his profound sympathy with the Southern States in their misfortunes. Indignantly he declared, that "second only to the wide-spread devastations of war were the robberies to which those States had been subjected, under an administration calling itself Republican, and with local governments deriving their animating impulse from the party in power; and that the people in these communities would have been less than men, if, sinking under the intolerable burden, they did not turn for help to a new party, promising honesty and reform."

He recalled the reiterated expression he had given to his sentiments, ever since the breaking out of the war; and closed the recital with these words: "Such is the simple and harmonious record, showing how from the beginning I was devoted to peace, how constantly I longed for reconciliation; how, with every measure of equal rights, this longing found utterance; how it became an essential part of my life; how I discarded all idea of vengeance and punishment; how reconstruction was, to my mind, a transition period, and how earnestly I looked forward to the day when, after the recognition of equal rights, the Republic should again be one in reality as in name. If there are any who ever maintained a policy of hate, I never was so minded; and now in protesting against any such policy, I act only in obedience to the irresistible promptings of my soul."

And well might he speak thus. Let the people of the

South hear what I say. They were wont to see in him only the implacable assailant of that peculiar institution, which was so closely interwoven with all their traditions and habits of life, that they regarded it as the very basis of their social and moral existence, as the source of their prosperity and greatness; the unsparing enemy of the Rebellion, whose success was to realize the fondest dreams of their ambition; the never-resting advocate of the grant of suffrage to the colored people, which they thought to be designed for their own degradation. Thus they had persuaded themselves that Charles Sumner was to them a relentless foe.

They did not know, as others knew, that he whom they cursed as their persecutor had a heart beating warmly and tenderly for all the human kind ; that the efforts of his life were unceasingly devoted to those whom he thought most in need of aid ; that in the slave he saw only the human soul, with its eternal title to the same right and dignity which he himself enjoyed ; that he assailed the slavemaster only as the oppressor who denied that right ; and that the former oppressor ceasing to be such, and being oppressed himself, could surely count upon the fulness of his active sympathy freely given in the spirit of equal justice ; that it was the religion of his life to protect the weak and oppressed against the strong, no matter who were the weak and oppressed, no matter who were the strong. They knew not, that while fiercely combating a wrong, there was not in his heart a spark of hatred even for the wrong-doer who hated him. They knew not how well he deserved the high homage involuntarily paid to him by a cartoon during the late presidential campaign,—a cartoon, designed to be malicious, which represented Charles Sumner strewing flowers on the grave of Preston Brooks. They foresaw not, that to welcome them back to the full brotherhood of the American people, he would expose himself to a blow, wounding him as cruelly as that which years ago levelled him to the ground in the Senate Chamber. And this new blow he received for them. The people of the South ignored this long. Now that he is gone, let them never forget it.

From Europe Mr. Sumner returned late in the fall of 1872, much strengthened, but far from being well. At the opening of the session he reintroduced two measures which, as he thought, should complete the record of his political life. One was his civil-rights bill, which had failed in the last Congress, and the other, a resolution providing that the names of the battles won over fellow-citizens in the war of the Rebellion, should be removed from the regimental colors of the army, and from the army register. It was in substance only a repetition of a resolution which he had introduced ten years before, in 1862, during the war, when the first names of victories were put on American battle-flags. This resolution called forth a new storm against him. It was denounced as an insult to the heroic soldiers of the Union, and a degradation of their victories and well-earned laurels. It was condemned as an unpatriotic act.

Charles Sumner insult the soldiers who had spilled their blood in a war for human rights! Charles Sumner degrade victories and depreciate laurels won for the cause of universal freedom! How strange an imputation!

Let the dead man have a hearing. This was his thought:

No civilized nation, from the republics of antiquity down to our days, ever thought it wise or patriotic to preserve in conspicuous and durable form the mementos of victories won over fellow-citizens in civil war. Why not? Because every citizen should feel himself with all others as the child of a common country, and not as a defeated foe. All civilized governments of our days have instinctively followed the same dictate of wisdom and patriotism. The Irishman, when fighting for old England at Waterloo, was not to behold on the red cross floating above him the name of the Boyne. The Scotch Highlander, when standing in the trenches of Sebastopol, was not by the colors of his regiment to be reminded of Culloden. No French soldier at Austerlitz or Solferino had to read upon the tricolor any reminiscence of the Vendée. No Hungarian at Sadowa was taunted by any Austrian banner with the surrender of Villagos. No German regiment, from Saxony or Hanover, charging under the iron hail of Gravelotte, was made to remember by words written on a Prussian standard that the black eagle had conquered them at Koniggratz and Langensalza. Should the son of South Carolina, when at some future day defending the Republic against some foreign foe, be reminded by an inscription on the colors floating over him, that under this flag the gun was fired that killed his father at Gettysburg? Should this great and enlightened Republic, proud of standing in the front of human progress, be less wise, less large-hearted, than the ancients were two thousand years ago, and the kingly governments of Europe are to-day? Let the battle-flags of the brave volunteers, which they brought home from the war with the glorious record of their victories, be preserved intact as a proud ornament of our State-Houses and armories. But let the colors of the army, under which the sons of all the States are to meet and mingle in common patriotism, speak of nothing but union, — not a union of conquerors and conquered, but a union which is the mother of all, equally tender to all, knowing of nothing but equality, peace and love among her children. Do you want conspicuous mementos of your victories? They are written upon the dusky brow of every freeman who was once a slave; they are written on the gate-posts of a restored Union; and the most glorious of all will be written on the faces of a contented people, reunited in common national pride.

Such were the sentiments which inspired that resolution. Such were the sentiments which called forth a storm of obloquy. Such were the sentiments for which the Legislature of Massachusetts passed a solemn resolution of censure upon Charles Sumner, — Massachusetts, his own Massachusetts, whom he loved so ardently with a filial love, — of whom he was so proud, who had honored him so much in days gone by, and whom he had so long and so faithfully labored to serve and to honor! Oh, those were evil days, that winter; days sad and dark, when he sat there in his lonesome chamber, unable to leave it, the world moving around him, and in it so much that was hostile, — and he prostrated by the tormenting disease, which had returned with fresh violence, — unable to defend himself, — and with this bitter arrow in his heart! Why was not that resolution held up to scorn and vituperation as an insult to the brave, and an unpatriotic act — why was he not attacked and condemned for it when he first offered it, ten years before, and when he was in the fulness of manhood and power? If not then, why now? Why now? I shall never forget the melancholy hours I sat with him, seeking to lift him up with cheering words, and he, — his frame for hours racked with excruciating pain, and then exhausted with suffering, — gloomily brooding over the thought that he might die so!

How thankful I am, how thankful every human soul in Massachusetts, how thankful every American must be, that he did not die then! — and, indeed, more than once, death seemed to be knocking at his door. How thankful that he was spared to see the day, when the people by striking developments were convinced that those who had acted as he did, had after all not been impelled by mere whims of vanity, or reckless ambition, or sinister designs, but had good and patriotic reasons for what they did; — when the heart of Massachusetts came back to him full of the old love and confidence, assuring him that he would again be her chosen son for her representative seat in the House of States; — when the lawgivers of the old Commonwealth, obeying an irresistible impulse of justice, wiped away from the records of the Legislature, and from the fair name of the State, that resolution of censure which had stung him so deeply, — and when returning vigor lifted him up, and a new sunburst of hope illumined his life! How thankful we all are that he lived that one year longer!

And yet, have you thought of it, if he had died in those dark days, when so many clouds hung over him, — would not then the much vilified man have been the same Charles Sumner, whose death but one year later afflicted millions of hearts with a pang of bereavement, whose praise is now on every lip for the purity of his life, for his fidelity to great principles, and for the loftiness of his patriotism? Was he not a year ago the same, the same in purpose, the same in principle, the same in character? What had he done then that so many who praise him to-day should have then disowned him? See what he had done. He had simply been true to his convictions of duty. He had approved and urged what he thought right, he had attacked and opposed what he thought wrong. To his convictions of duty he had sacrificed political associations most dear to him, the security of his position of which he was proud. For his convictions of duty he had stood up against those more powerful than he; he had exposed himself to reproach, obloquy and persecution. Had he not done so, he would not have been the man you praise to-day; and yet for doing so he was cried down but yesterday. He had lived up to the great word he spoke when he entered the Senate: "The slave of principle, I call no party master." That declaration was greeted with applause, and when, true to his word, he refused to call a party master, the act was covered with reproach.

The spirit impelling him to do so was the same conscience which urged him to break away from the powerful party which controlled his State in the days of Daniel Webster, and to join a feeble minority, which stood up for freedom; to throw away the favor and defy the power of the wealthy and refined, in order to plead the cause of the down-trodden and degraded; to stand up against the slave power in Congress with a courage never surpassed; to attack the prejudice of birth and religion, and to plead fearlessly for the rights of the foreign-born citizen at a time when the know-nothing movement was controlling his State and might have defeated his own re-election to the Senate; to advocate emancipation when others trembled with fear; to march ahead of his followers, when they were afraid to follow; to rise up alone for what he thought right, when others would not rise with him. It was that brave spirit which does everything, defies everything, risks everything, sacrifices everything, comfort, society, party, popular support, station of honor, prospects, for sense of right and conviction of duty. That is it for which you honored him long, for which you reproached him yesterday, and for which you honor him again to-day, and will honor him forever.

Ah, what a lesson is this for the American people, — a lesson learned so often, and, alas! forgotten almost as often as it is learned! Is it well to discourage, to proscribe in your public men that independent spirit which will boldly assert a conscientious sense of duty, even against the behests of power or party? Is it well to teach them that they must serve the command and interest of party, even at the price of conscience, or they must be crushed under its heel, whatever their past service, whatever their ability, whatever their character may be? Is it well to make them believe that he who dares to be himself must be hunted as a political outlaw, who will find justice only when he is dead? That would have been the sad moral of his death, had Charles Sumner died a year ago.

Let the American people never forget that it has always been the independent spirit, the all-defying sense of duty which broke the way for every great progressive movement since mankind has a history; which gave the American colonies their sovereignty and made this great Republic; which defied the power of slavery, and made this a Republic of freemen; and which — who knows, — may again be needed some day to defy the power of ignorance, to arrest the inroads of corruption, or to break the subtle tyranny of organization in order to preserve this as a Republic! And therefore let no man understand me as offering what I have said about Mr. Sumner's course, during the last period of his life, as an apology for what he did. He was right before his own conscience, and needs no apology. Woe to the Republic when it looks in vain for the men who seek the truth without prejudice and speak the truth without fear, as they understand it, no matter whether the world be willing to listen or not! Alas for the generation that would put such men into their graves with the poor boon of an apology for what was in them noblest and best! Who will not agree that, had power or partisan spirit, which persecuted him because he followed higher aims than party interest, ever succeeded in subjugating and moulding him after its fashion, against his conscience, against his conviction of duty, against his sense of right, he would have sunk into his grave a miserable ruin of his great self, wrecked in his moral nature, deserving only a tear of pity? For he was great and useful only because he dared to be himself all the days of his life; and for this you have, when he died, put the laurel upon his brow!

From the coffin which hides his body, Charles Sumner now rises up before our eyes an historic character. Let us look at him once more. His life lies before us like an open book which contains no double meanings, no crooked passages, no mysteries, no concealments. It is clear as crystal.

Even his warmest friend will not see in it the model of perfect statesmanship; not that eagle glance which, from a lofty eminence, at one sweep surveys the whole field on which by labor, thought, strife, accommodation, impulse, restraint, slow and rapid movement, the destinies of a nation are worked out, — and which, while surveying the whole, yet observes and penetrates the fitness and working of every detail of the great machinery; — not that ever calm and steady and self-controlling good sense, which judges existing things just as they are, and existing forces just as to what they can accomplish, and while instructing, conciliating, persuading and moulding those forces, and guiding them on toward an ideal end, correctly estimates comparative good and comparative evil, and impels or restrains as that estimate may command. That is the true genius of statesmanship, fitting all times, all circumstances, and all great objects to be reached by political action.

Mr. Sumner's natural abilities were not of the very first order; but they were supplemented by acquired abilities of most remarkable power. His mind was not apt to invent and create by inspiration; it produced by study and work. Neither had his mind superior constructive capacity. When he desired to originate a measure of legislation, he scarcely ever elaborated its practical detail; he usually threw his idea into the form of a resolution, or a bill giving in the main his purpose only, and then he advanced to the discussion of the principles involved. It was difficult for him to look at a question or problem from more than one point of view, and to comprehend its different bearings, its complex relations with other questions or problems; and to that one point of view he was apt to subject all other considerations. He not only thought, but he did not hesitate to say that all construction of the Constitution must be subservient to the supreme duty of giving the amplest protection to the natural rights of man by direct national legislation. He was not free from that dangerous tendency to forget the limits which bound the legitimate range of legislative and governmental action. On economical questions his views were enlightened and thoroughly consistent. He had studied such subjects more than is commonly supposed. It was one of his last regrets that his health did not permit him to make a speech in favor of an early resumption of specie payments. On matters of international law and foreign affairs he was the recognized authority of the Senate.

But some of his very shortcomings served to increase that peculiar power which he exerted in his time. His public life was thrown into a period of a revolutionary character, when one great end was the self-imposed subject of a universal struggle, a struggle which was not made, not manufactured by the design of men, but had grown from the natural conflict of existing things, and grew irresistibly on and on, until it enveloped all the thought of the nation; and that one great end appealing more than to the practical sense, to the moral impulses of men, making of them the fighting force. There Mr. Sumner found his place and there he grew great, for that moral impulse was stronger in him than in most of the world around him; and it was in him not a mere crude, untutored force of nature, but educated and elevated by thought and study; and it found in his brain and heart an armory of strong weapons given to but few: vast information, legal learning, industry, eloquence, undaunted courage, an independent and iron will, profound convictions, unbounded devotion and sublime faith. It found there also a keen and just instinct as to the objects which must be reached and the forces which must be set in motion and driven on to reach them. Thus keeping the end steadily, obstinately, intensely in view, he marched ahead of his followers, never disturbed by their anxieties and fears, showing them that what was necessary was possible, and forcing them to follow him, — a great moving power, such as the struggle required.

Nor can it be said that this impatient, irrepressible propulsion was against all prudence and sound judgment, for it must not be forgotten, that, when Mr. Sumner stepped into the front, the policy of compromise was exhausted; the time of composition and expedient was past. Things had gone so far, that the idea of reaching the end, which ultimately must be reached, by mutual concession and a gradual and peaceable process, was utterly hopeless. The conflicting forces could not be reconciled; the final struggle was indeed irrepressible and inevitable, and all that could then be done was to gather up all the existing forces for one supreme effort, and to take care that the final struggle should bring forth the necessary results.

Thus the instinct and the obstinate, concentrated, irresistible moving power which Mr. Sumner possessed were an essential part of the true statesmanship of the revolutionary period. Had he lived before or after this great period, in quiet, ordinary times, he would perhaps never have gone into public life, or never risen in it to conspicuous significance. But all he was by nature, by acquirement, by ability, by moral impulse, made him one of the heroes of that great struggle against slavery, and in some respects the first. And then when the victory was won, the same moral nature, the same sense of justice, the same enlightened mind, impelled him to plead the cause of peace, reconciliation and brotherhood, through equal rights and even justice, thus completing the fulness of his ideal. On the pedestal of his time he stands one of the greatest of Americans.

What a peculiar power of fascination there was in him as a public man! It acted much through his eloquence, but not through his eloquence alone. His speech was not a graceful flow of melodious periods, now drawing on the listener with the persuasive tone of confidential conversation, then carrying him along with a more rapid rush of thought and language, and at last lifting him up with the peals of reason in passion. His arguments marched forth at once in grave and stately array; his sentences like rows of massive doric columns, unrelieved by pleasing variety, severe and imposing. His orations, especially those pronounced in the Senate before the war, contain many passages of grandest beauty. There was nothing kindly persuasive in his utterance; his reasoning appeared in the form of consecutive assertion, not seldom strictly logical and irresistibly strong. His mighty appeals were always addressed to the noblest instincts of human nature. His speech was never enlivened by anything like wit or humor. They were foreign to his nature. He has never been guilty of a flash of irony or sarcasm. His weapon was not the foil, but the battle-axe.

He has often been accused of being uncharitable to opponents in debate, and of wounding their feelings with uncalled for harshness of language. He was guilty of that, but no man was less conscious of the stinging force of his language than he. He was often sorry for the effect his thrusts had produced, but being always so firmly and honestly persuaded of the correctness of his own opinions, that he could scarcely ever appreciate the position of an opponent, he fell into the same fault again. Not seldom he appeared haughty in his assumptions of authority; but it was the imperiousness of profound conviction, which, while sometimes exasperating his hearers, yet scarcely ever failed to exercise over them a certain sway. His fancy was not fertile, his figures mostly labored and stiff. In his later years his vast learning began to become an encumbering burden to his eloquence. The mass of quoted sayings and historical illustrations, not seldom accumulated beyond measure and grotesquely grouped, sometimes threatened to suffocate the original thought and to oppress the hearer. But even then his words scarcely ever failed to chain the attention of the audience, and I have more than once seen the Senate attentively listening while he read from printed slips the most elaborate disquisition, which, if attempted by any one of his colleagues, would at once have emptied the floor and galleries. But there were always moments recalling to our mind the days of his freshest vigor, when he stood in the midst of the great struggle, lifting up the youth of the country with heart-stirring appeals, and with the lion-like thunder of his voice shaking the Senate chamber.

Still there was another source from which that fascination sprung. Behind all he said and did there stood a grand manhood, which never failed to make itself felt. What a figure he was, with his tall and stalwart frame, his manly face, topped with his shaggy locks, his noble bearing, the finest type of American Senatorship, the tallest oak of the forest! And how small they appeared by his side, the common run of politicians, who spend their days with the laying of pipe, and the setting up of pins, and the pulling of wires; who barter an office to secure this vote, and procure a contract to get that; who stand always with their ears to the wind to hear how the administration sneezes, and what their constituents whisper, in mortal trepidation lest they fail in being all things to everybody! How he towered above them, he whose aims were always the highest and noblest; whose very presence made you forget the vulgarities of political life; who dared to differ with any man ever so powerful, any multitude ever so numerous; who regarded party as nothing but a means for great ends, and for those ends defied its power; to whom the arts of demagogism were so contemptible, that he would rather have sunk into obscurity and oblivion than descend to them; to whom the dignity of his office was so sacred that he would not even ask for it for fear of darkening its lustre!

Honor to the people of Massachusetts who, for twenty-three years, kept in the Senate, and would have kept him there ever so long, had he lived, a man who never, even to them, conceded a single iota of his convictions in order to remain there! And what a life was his! A life so wholly devoted to what was good and pure! There he stood in the midst of the grasping materialism of our times, around him the eager chase for the almighty dollar, no thought of opportunity ever entering the smallest corner of his mind, and disturbing his high endeavors; with a virtue which the possession of power could not even tempt, much less debauch; from whose presence the very thought of corruption instinctively shrunk back; a life so spotless, an integrity so intact, a character so high, that the most daring eagerness of calumny, the most wanton audacity of insinuation, standing on tiptoe, could not touch the soles of his shoes!

They say that he indulged in overweening self-appreciation. Ay, he did have a magnificent pride, a lofty self-esteem. Why should he not? Let wretches despise themselves, for they have good reason to do so; not he. But in his self-esteem there was nothing small and mean; no man lived to whose very nature envy and petty jealousy were more foreign. Conscious of his own merit, he never depreciated the merit of others; nay, he not only recognized it, but he expressed that recognition with that cordial spontaneity which can only flow from a sincere and generous heart. His pride of self was like his pride of country. He was the proudest American; he was the proudest New Englander; and yet he was the most cosmopolitan American I have ever seen. There was in him not the faintest shadow of that narrow prejudice which looks askance at what has grown in foreign lands. His generous heart and his enlightened mind were too generous and too enlightened not to give the fullest measure of appreciation to all that was good and worthy, from whatever quarter of the globe it came.

And now his home! There are those around me who have breathed the air of his house in Washington, that atmosphere of refinement, taste, scholarship, art, friendship, and warm-hearted hospitality; who have seen those rooms covered and filled with his pictures, his engravings, his statues, his bronzes, his books and rare manuscripts — the collections of a lifetime — the image of the richness of his mind, the comfort and consolation of his solitude. They have beheld his childlike smile of satisfaction when he unlocked the most precious of his treasures and told their stories.

They remember the conversations at his hospitable board, genially inspired and directed by him, on art and books and inventions and great times and great men, — when suddenly sometimes, by accident, a new mine of curious knowledge disclosed itself in him, which his friends had never known he possessed; or when a sunburst of the affectionate gentleness of his soul warmed all hearts around him. They remember his craving for friendship, as it spoke through the far outstretched hand when you arrived, and the glad exclamation: "I am so happy you came," — and the beseeching, almost despondent tone when you departed: "Do not leave me yet; do stay a while longer, I want so much to speak with you!" — It is all gone now. He could not stay himself, and he has left his friends behind, feeling more deeply than ever that no man could know him well but to love him.

Now we have laid him into his grave, in the motherly soil of Massachusetts, which was so dear to him. He is at rest now, the stalwart, brave old champion, whose face and bearing were so austere, and whose heart was so full of tenderness; who began his career with a pathetic plea for universal peace and charity, and whose whole life was an arduous, incessant, never-resting struggle, which left him all covered with scars. And we can do nothing for him but commemorate his lofty ideals of Liberty, and Equality, and Justice, and Reconciliation, and Purity, and the earnestness and courage and touching fidelity with which he fought for them; so genuine in his sincerity, so single-minded in his zeal, so heroic in his devotion!

Oh, that we could but for one short hour call him up from his coffin, to let him see with the same eyes which saw so much hostility, that those who stood against him in the struggles of his life are his enemies no longer! That we could show him the fruit of the conflicts and sufferings of his last three years, and that he had not struggled and suffered in vain! We would bring before him, not only those who from offended partisan zeal assailed him, and who now with sorrowful hearts praise the purity of his patriotism; but we would bring to him that man of the South, a slaveholder and a leader of secession in his time, the echo of whose words spoken in the name of the South in the halls of the National Capitol we heard but yesterday; words of respect, of gratitude, of tenderness. That man of the South should then do what he deplored not to have done while he lived,— he should lay his hand upon the shoulders of the old friend of the human kind and say to him: "Is it you whom I hated, and who, as I thought, hated me? I have learned now the greatness and magnanimity of your soul, and here I offer you my hand and heart."

Could he but see this with those eyes, so weary of contention and strife, how contentedly would he close them again, having beheld the greatness of his victories!

People of Massachusetts! he was the son of your soil, in which he now sleeps; but he is not all your own. He belongs to all of us in the North and in the South,—to the blacks he helped to make free, and to the whites he strove to make brothers again. On the grave of him whom so many thought to be their enemy, and found to be their friend, let the hands be clasped which so bitterly warred against each other. Upon that grave let the youth of America be taught, by the story of his life, that not only genius, power and success, but more than these, patriotic devotion and virtue, make the greatness of the citizen! If this lesson be understood and followed, more than Charles Sumner's living word could have done for the glory of America will then be done by the inspiration of his great example. And it will truly be said, that although his body lies mouldering in the earth, yet in the assured rights of all, in the brotherhood of a reunited people, and in a purified Republic, he still lives and will live forever.

Printed in Dunstable, United Kingdom